Chaos in the Classroom

CHAOS IN THE CLASSROOM

A New Theory of Teaching and Learning

Elizabeth Jane Davis
Thomas J. Smith
Dorothy Leflore

CAROLINA ACADEMIC PRESS
Durham, North Carolina

Library of Congress Cataloging-in-Publication Data
Davis, Elizabeth Jane, 1936-
Chaos in the classroom : a new theory of teaching and learning /
by Elizabeth Jane Davis, Thomas J. Smith, Dorothy Leflore.
    p. cm.
Includes bibliographical references and index.
ISBN 10: 1-59460-407-X
ISBN 13: 978-1-59460-407-2 (alk. paper)
1. Learning. 2. Cognition in children. I. Smith, Thomas J.
(Thomas Jean), 1949- II. Leflore, Dorothy, 1944- III. Title.

LB1060.D384 2007
370.15'23--dc22

                                                    2007031323

CAROLINA ACADEMIC PRESS
700 Kent Street
Durham, North Carolina 27701
Telephone (919) 489-7486
Fax (919) 493-5668
www.cap-press.com

Printed in the United States of America

CONTENTS

INTRODUCTION

Dr. Lelia Vickers
Dean, School of Education
North Carolina A&T State University

This book, *Chaos in the Classroom*, considers what most researchers may not, that there is a definitive relationship between chaos theory, critical thinking, and brain research. While others have attempted to examine one of these ideas, Davis, Smith, and Leflore advocate that a definitive relationship exists between these three concepts and that this relationship has a positive impact upon students in classrooms. There are numerous theories that consider how students learn, but chaos theory is one of those that many educators have not sought to understand, let alone implement in educational settings.

Many educators still rely upon a linearly reductive conception of cognition that posits knowledge to be independent and external to the student's reality. Such a worldview mandates that teachers insert knowledge into the minds of the students in the most effective and efficient method possible, irrespective of context. Therefore, conceptualization is inhibited and students are assessed on their ability to memorize, but not utilize, knowledge.

The authors have chosen to advance a theory not readily employed in the classroom that, when implemented, connects with the nonlinear structure of our brain. If one considers Gardner's theory of multiple intelligences, it is quite clear that educators have focused too long on the notion that one size fits all.

The approach Davis, Smith, and Leflore take in linking brain research to learning is not novel; however, brain research has not been readily applied in instructional settings or in the development of materials for teaching higher-order thinking skills. Perhaps higher-order thinking skills are not as difficult to teach when they are taught in an instructional setting that allows students, not their teachers, to employ specific learning modalities. The authors are able to demonstrate that the highly organized linear approach to learning might be just the opposite of what most students actually need. Students learn according to their experiences, and since we live in a chaotic (not linear) environment, structured chaos can be successfully employed in the classroom.

The new theory of cognition advocated by Davis, Smith, and Leflore correlates to the "Mozart Effect" based on the research of Rauscher and Shaw (1993) that suggested that listening to Mozart's *Sonata for Two Pianos in D Major* could causally enhance the child's ability to create, maintain, transform, and relate complex mental images through time. It is exactly this type of reasoning that is involved when learning mathematics, science, physics, and chess.

The authors encourage the reader to step outside his/her comfort zone to consider the uniqueness of experience. For example, students who participate in the same group discussion will derive their own unique conclusions because everybody has had their own unique experiences prior to the discussion. Additionally, each student will have had a unique experience during the discussion; thus each student's conclusion is justifiable. Experiences must, therefore, be the primary focus in the teaching process. Teaching is a complex endeavor. While we understand some of the components of teaching and learning, according to the theory of chaos, there are numerous variables that influence whether or not a learner will master a specific concept. Unlike linear learning, which is teacher-centered, the experience of the learner will determine whether or not a concept is worth remembering. In a teacher-centered classroom there is only one correct answer; in a student-centered classrooms answers are multiple and all are correct. Student-centered learning focuses upon critical thinking from multiple and diverse perspectives. Based upon the interest and the experience of the learner, it is the natural way to learn. Therefore, the teacher must change his/her role from one who is the intellectual boss of the classroom to one who employs a variety of pedagogical modalities that address the individual experiences of the learners. Thus, chaos is the only way to learn.

Rauscher F.H., Shaw G.L., Ky K.N. Music and spatial task performance, *Nature* 1993; 365:611.

Chaos in the Classroom

CHAPTER 1

THE NONLINEAR DYNAMIC THEORY OF LEARNING

A New Theory

For the first time since the late 1980s, a new way of looking at learning and its relationship to teaching has been proposed. It takes into account the most recent research in brain-based learning theory, social constructivist learning theory, multiple intelligence theory and chaos theory. It sheds new light on the observed processes in the classroom that promote deep understanding and affords teachers a new way of planning and managing these processes.

Learning theories developed rapidly during the 1960s and 1970s for several reasons. Those theories that were based on studies of animals were found to be wanting in several areas, especially in the areas of motivation. While animals respond well to extrinsic motivation, it was discovered that children, over time, do not. In fact, extrinsic motivation seemed to have an opposite effect on learning. Other theories that seemed to take into account intrinsic motivation were still teacher-centered and teacher controlled, and tended to have short-term results. Constructivist learning theory seems to have the most promising results, especially long-term effects, but requires that teachers relinquish much of their control, and thus tends to be misunderstood by the profession at large. The new theory proposed by the authors is grounded in constructivist theory, brings critical thinking into the constructivist paradigm, and incorporates current brain research. This is viewed through the lens of chaos theory, and makes understandable many of the long-term effects of the learning/teaching process.

Why Do We Need a New Theory of Learning?

Developing learners who are strong critical thinkers has been put forth as a major goal for school systems which seek to graduate students who can deal with a changing world and who can make an impact on this world in a positive, productive way. Today it is imperative that teachers not only be made aware of this movement, but also be taught how to recognize critical thinking when it occurs. It is included in the INTASC principles that specify what beginning teachers should know and be able to do, and in the standards that must be met for National Board Certification. In addition, current research in brain-based learning has established evidence that many traditional classroom practices such as concentrating on rote memorization and not allowing students adequate water and movement can actually damage the brain and prevent it from developing to greater potential.

Many of the current learning theories such as behavioral learning theory, cognitive learning theory and social learning theory focus on the teaching of skills in a teacher-controlled environment. Even when students are given choices, these choices are not really their decisions, but instead are given to them by the teacher. Inquiry lessons that are used as models for critical thinking often begin with an "essential question" posed by the teacher. And, especially in the behaviorist paradigm, critical thinking skills are taught and required to be mastered before students are allowed to exercise them on their own. Further, the "at-risk" students who are most in need of critical thinking skills are often excluded from those allowed to do it because they "haven't earned the right" to do so, either on behavioral terms or on academic terms.

Davis-Seaver (2001) found that children think critically very well, but that they do it most often outside of school, or in school when they think no one is noticing. She found that "good thinking" was equated with doing what the teacher told them to do, and with getting the "right" (the teacher's) answer.

This new theory explains how working with the way the brain learns naturally and using critical thinking to develop knowledge of content will turn this situation around and convince students that learning is a worthwhile activity, that the challenges of substantial inquiry and the pleasure of discovery are theirs to control throughout their lives. This theory also looks at the environment of a brain-friendly classroom and gives teachers sound educational theory for a variety of pedagogical strategies. In subsequent chapters, the authors will discuss actual classrooms that operate in a chaotic environment and benefit educationally, socially and physically from the experience.

Beginning with Critical Thinking for Every Child

Critical thinking goes beyond the "worksheet mentality" found too often especially in elementary schools, where "skills" are taught, rote memory is encouraged, and students are praised for coming up with the "right" (that is, the teacher's) answer. It involves creativity, flexibility, risk taking, and an interdisciplinary approach to learning, both on the part of the student and the teacher. In other words, the brains of both student and teacher are highly involved and active.

As Richard Paul, Director of the Center for Critical Thinking at Sonoma State University, California, says in describing himself as a critical thinker,

> I can't be inflexibly attached to any particular beliefs. I strive for a consistent "big picture." I approach other perspectives differently. I ask how I can reconcile the points of view. I see variations between similar but different perspectives. I use principles and insights flexibly, and do not approach analysis as a mechanical, step one, step two process. I pursue new ideas in depth, trying to understand the perspectives from which they come. I am willing to say "This view sounds new and different, I don't yet understand it. There's more to this idea than I realized, I can't just dismiss it." (Paul, p. iv)

Vera John-Steiner, in exploring the thinking strategies of many of the world's greatest thinkers, says,

> Of greatest importance in the thought activity of artists and scientists is their pulling together of ideas, images, disarrayed facts and fragments of experience, which have previously been apprehended by them as separated in time and space, into an integrated work. It is this synthesis that most concerns

me in this discussion: the joining of rapid bursts of thought with a regime of disciplined work (John-Steiner, p. 77)

Paul also says that these same characteristics should be found in teachers who value critical thinking in their classrooms so they can model for students the critical thinking they are trying to develop in them. He explains further, that

> The teacher who teaches students how to learn and think about many basic issues gives them knowledge they can use the rest of their lives. This teacher realizes that subject matter divisions are arbitrary and a matter of convenience. She realizes that the most important problems of everyday life rarely fall neatly into subject matter divisions, that understanding a situation fully usually requires a synthesis of knowledge and insight from several subjects. (Paul, p. 9)

Pursuing the goal of making critical thinking a way of understanding the curriculum of the elementary school classroom and taking the perspective that critical, in-depth thinking necessarily must be interdisciplinary and compatible with current brain research, the new theory of learning encompasses a new way of looking at the learning process and the environment that is required for in-depth understanding to take place.

It develops the idea that an environment that fosters critical thinking is multilevel and diverse, with as many different perspectives as there are students and teachers who are members of the learning community. Further, it is impossible to think critically without actively using the brain and without creating new neural pathways and dendritic connections in the brain.

This new theory is viewed through the lens of chaos theory, and presents a revolutionary pedagogical stance that represents a major change in paradigm rather than merely revising or "tweaking" what is already in place. As James Gleick says, "Often a revolution has an interdisciplinary character—its central discoveries often come from people straying outside the normal bounds of their specialties." (Gleick, p. 37)

Close attention to classroom dynamics and teaching methods reveals that the traditional didactic teaching strategies are inadequate to accomplish this change, and thus the turn to disciplines that ordinarily deal with diversity, change, synthesis and turbulence; that is, those of physics, meteorology, neuroscience and mathematics, specifically the study of nonlinearity in dynamic systems.

When faced with the prospect of diversity and turbulence in the classroom as a method of fostering creativity and critical thinking, many teachers respond, "That would be pure chaos."

Exactly.

Chaos Theory As a Window to the Learning Process

What do sciences as far away from an elementary school classroom as meteorology, economics, cardiology and physics have to tell us about the practical, day-to-day experience of fostering creative, independent critical thinking among students? They tell us that processes, whether they are in fluid dynamics, population growth, stock market prices, or fibrillation are nonlinear processes that obey universal principles of chaos.

Investigating such processes and linking them to the creative and critical thinking processes of children in the elementary school classroom requires not an examination of the definitions of critical thinking, which are well established, but instead an examination of chaotic dynamics and their application to the brain-based learning process of critical and creative thinking. Petree reports

> Ott, Grebogi and Yorke cited the many purposes of chaos and said it might even be necessary in higher life forms for brain functioning. Freeman studied just such brain functions related to the olfactory system and concluded that indeed chaos "affords an opportunity to exploit further these manifestations of brain activities." (Petree, p. 5)

In educational terms, that means that teachers must realize that education is a nonlinear process, where input does not equal output, where cause is widely separated from effect, and time is one-directional. Learning therefore cannot be broken down into its component parts, analyzed, and then be reassembled into a whole. The parts won't fit. In the process of compartmentalizing learning into fragments of subject matter, thinking about basic concepts and transfer of these concepts is lost, and the educator who assumes that parts always add up to a whole and who forecasts successful readers by teaching skills in isolation will often get students who are "word callers," and have no idea what those words mean.

Chaos has randomness and complexity, jagged edges and sudden leaps; it speculates about determinism and free will, evolution and conscious intelligence. In other words, chaos presents a picture of true learning as a process. To paraphrase Joseph Ford, a physicist at Georgia Institute of Technology, chaos, educationally speaking is thinking freed from the shackles of order and predictability, children liberated to explore their every dynamical possibility, resulting in exciting variety, richness of ideas and thought, a cornucopia of opportunity.

Whether looking at the education of a single child or at a whole group of children, viewing the process as nonlinear lets the teacher see that chaos, or learning in discrete time units (the leaps and jagged edges) and learning holistically rather than in fragmented, isolated units, are a part of the entire process of education, and that the turbulence of divergent ideas and solutions is the key to creative critical thinking, and that without this chaos in the classroom, true education does not take place.

Sensitive Dependence on Initial Conditions

Important to our understanding of chaos and its relevance to classroom dynamics is a knowledge of sensitive dependence on initial conditions; that is, small variances that multiply and at later points magnify to a point of crisis, or chaos. In this case, crisis does not imply an emergency situation. It implies instead a catastrophe shelf or a bifurcation point. This is better known as the butterfly effect, cited by Edward Lorenz, a meteorologist, who said that the flapping of a butterfly's wings in Brazil could cause tornados in Texas next week.

Educationally speaking, the investigation of dinosaurs in second grade can lead to a Ph.D. in anthropology later, which can result in groundbreaking research in paleontology. Or, the linking of math and science in a project in fifth grade can lead to sudden insight into the way numbers and charts and graphs guide the understanding of the way our society works in the real world.

On a less positive but important note, sensitive dependence on initial conditions can explain what we now call the problem learner, or at-risk child. A child enters school in a classroom where certain knowledge is a given for most of the students, and because it takes time to create the necessary schema to embed the new knowledge that is being given to her, she ends the first year of school in a far different state of understanding than her peers.

Another aspect of sensitive dependence on initial conditions is that of intelligences and learning styles. In a classroom that favors verbal/linguistic and logical/mathematical intelligences over any other, and mastery learning styles over any other (which are the majority of classrooms today) a student who enters the learning process through another intelligence and/or uses a learning style not valued, is highly likely to have a vastly different learning experience than others in the classroom. In the view of most brain-based learning researchers, this destroys neural pathways, causes a sloughing off of brain cells, and does actual damage to the developing brain of a student. Further, any classroom that does not utilize the full strength of the brain to engage the student in the learning process by appealing to critical thinking as a way of understanding curriculum does further damage by creating neural pathways that lead to habits of learning that are at the lowest level of Bloom's taxonomy, e.g. memorization of discrete facts. Because the brain categorizes and embeds new information within schema or categories, the lack of categories, or the lack of the choice to use a preferred intelligence for processing new information either by accommodation or assimilation will result in either the embedding of the new information into inappropriate schema and therefore a complete misunderstanding of the concept, or the refusal of the brain to embed the information anywhere.

Critical thinking begins with an examination of the assumptions that students have about a concept with the purpose of understanding underlying feelings and thoughts that influence what they already know or think they know. Brain-based learning research has established that emotions are critical to learning, and emotions can greatly influence the process of assimilation and accommodation where existing schema are expanded, in the case of assimilation, or changed, in the case of accommodation. Problem solving begins with the questions, "What is the problem?" and "What information do I have?" Students who are used to being given this information develop the habit of not examining assumptions and feelings underlying these assumptions, and therefore lose the opportunity to develop an in-depth understanding of the concept.

Using knowledge of sensitive dependence on initial conditions in the classroom through such strategies as a KWL chart to access prior knowledge enables a teacher to create choices for students that will use their already created schema, and she can facilitate the processes of accommodation and assimilation that are necessary for understanding. Further, by allowing student choices in the methods they use to process their knowledge, and by valuing their choices, the teacher can begin to understand the diversity of learning styles and intelligences that her students have, and can use this to create rich, varied and interdisciplinary units of study that are student-directed and student controlled, thereby maximizing the learning that takes place.

Iteration

Iteration is the driving force of the chaotic dynamics of nonlinear systems. It is a simple repeating of a certain function or action, using previous output as input for the next action. For example, using a calculator that will iterate, you can put in a number such as 2, the function of times 2, press equal and get 4. If you press equal again, the calculator iterates the function of times 2, and now the answer is 8. It used the output of the first iteration, 4, as input for the second iteration of times 2. Do this again and you will get 16 because the function of times 2 was applied to the previous output of 8.

A familiar classroom example is that of the hyperactive child who spends a great deal of the school day in suspension and misses most of his reading instruction time. Since he cannot read, he becomes more disruptive, especially during reading time when others are engaged in an activity that excludes him, and is thereupon sent out to more suspension, where he falls further behind in reading. His initial condition of hyperactivity has now been iterated into a reading problem, and he becomes the victim of functional iteration, a feed-back loop. His behavioral handicap now is compounded by the additional handicap of illiteracy. Should this condition not be understood by the teacher, this situation can iterate into dropping out of school.

On the other hand, iterations are just as often a creative process. Gleick reminds us that

> The heart of the snowflake model is the essence of chaos; a delicate balance between forces of stability and instability ... (it) serves not to destroy but to create ... The final flake records the history of all the changing weather conditions it has experienced and the combinations may as well be infinite. (Gleick, pp. 309–11)

Theodor Swenk in "Das Sensible Chaos" (1965) (as cited in Gleick) spoke to the creative force of turbulence in water. His idea was that vortices were caused by inequalities and these inequalities could be those of any medium "could be fast and slow, warm and cold, dense and tenuous, viscous and fluid, acid and alkaline. At the boundary, life blossoms." (Gleick, p. 198) He could just as well have been addressing the development of creative and critical thinking in the classroom. Inequalities, that is divergent ideas, many points of view, create whorls and eddies of ideas and as they play upon each other, critical thinking develops—the structure within chaos seen by scientists and educators alike. The initial conditions of diversity, whether from intelligences, learning styles, or prior knowledge, when iterated create a rich and varied learning experience that is infinite in its possibilities.

Students, like snowflakes, are nonequilibrium phenomena, products of imbalance in the flow and reception of learning experiences, and obeying the universal principles of chaos, each one is unique. Current brain research has shown that this is true of brains as well as minds. In education, it is imperative that we realize that feeding any one group of children, no matter how homogeneous we think they are, the same diet of information will not result in every child in that group learning the same thing. The principles of chaos take effect just as surely as they do in the fields of mathematics, physics, economics and biology. Because of sensitive dependence on initial conditions; that is, because of the butterfly effect of where each child is individually and its unique experiences within its own life, each child gets a unique learning experience from each exposure (iteration) to learning. This explains why we get the many individual responses to a shared experience in the classroom; a condition, chaotic in nature that amazes and delights the teacher who is attuned to critical and creative thinking, as it does the scientist who finds beauty and excitement in the turbulence of the waterfall or Mandelbrot's set of complex numbers.

It seems apparent that truly creative, independent, critical thinking is created by the conflicting pulls of divergent ideas. John-Steiner examined this idea in her research into creative thinking processes. She found

> The contradictory movements by which creative work might progress was noted by the psychologist Rudolf Arnheim. He studied Picasso's sketches and photographs of the developing painting "Guernica" and found that the painter proceeded through many erratic leaps as well as modifications and compensations before he achieved the desired unity of composition that distinguished the finished painting ... The essence of dialectical thinking is to find in each case what are the oppositions, conflicts, contrasts, contradictions, the otherness, estrangement, alienation that are possible in the context and to find the notion that unites them by incorporating and using rather than destroying their tension. (John-Steiner, p. 137)

Gleick says that

> Those studying chaotic dynamics discovered that the disorderly behavior of simple systems acted as a creative process. It generated complexity; richly organized patterns sometimes stable and sometimes unstable, sometimes finite and sometimes infinite, but always with the fascination of living things. (Gleick, p. 43)

This process of dialectical and dialogical thinking that characterizes critical thinking is one of iteration, that is, of using the thoughts and ideas of one person as input for the next thoughts and ideas about a concept, and which sometimes lead to consensus or common solution or answer, or sometimes lead to a variety of solutions and answers, all of which are valid and which open up possibilities for other solutions and answers.

Self-Similarity (Fractals), Catastrophe Shelves, Density and Strange Attractors

Many years ago, Aristotle posited that physical motion is not a quantity or a force, but a process, a kind of change, and as such, subject to chaos. So too is critical thinking a process, a kind of change and also subject to chaos. Richard Paul addresses this when he states

> I ... realize that my perspective has changed. Perhaps I recall learning a new idea or even system of thought that changed the way I see myself and the world around me in fundamental ways, perhaps changed my life ... I realize that I now have a new choice regarding the issue under scrutiny ... I realize I can make my point of view richer so it encompasses more. One of the most important stages in my development as a thinker, then is a clear recognition that I have a perspective, one that I must work on and change as I learn and grow. (Paul, pp. iii–iv)

Gleick understands this property of creative change as part of the robustness of a chaotic system. He explains that chaotic systems are robust, that is, stability and instability exist together; a chaotic system is stable if its instability or irregularity persists in the face of small disturbances; that is, locally unpredictable but globally stable. This applies to critical thinking in the classroom in that each student may be thinking any one of many different thoughts, and any number of thoughts may be arrived at from any number of perceptions, but globally, the thoughts are arrived at, are created; thinking is achieved. Several students may, together or independently, arrive at the same thought, while the rest of the class arrives at x number of various thoughts. These thoughts change creatively as this process is occurring because of local disturbances, that is, internalizing of new, different perspectives affecting previously held beliefs, which are un-predictable in advance, but which do not affect the global outcome which is critical thinking about an issue or concept.

Part of the problem with understanding and fostering creative, critical thinking in the classroom is that we have been looking at this type of thinking linearly. That is, we have been using "differential equation kinds of analysis" to describe the intake/output of the educational process and then when it doesn't work out, we have tried another differential equation type analysis instead of finding another type of equation altogether. A differential equation describes processes that change smoothly over time, says Gleick. He suggests using difference equations for processes that "jump from state to state," such as chaotic dynamic systems. This makes sense also in describing learning processes.

We know that children make sudden leaps and bounds in learning, that progress is erratic, going forward, then backwards, then remaining still—yet we teach as though they make smooth progress over time. Our predictions about children's learning thus break down over time. We have been using differential equation thinking when we should have been using difference equation thinking, a new way of looking at the educational process altogether.

Part of this new way of looking at education and brain-based critical thinking involves understanding the phase space of the classroom and the presence of the strange attractor there. A strange attractor is the map of the movement of a process through time space. A strange attractor can be graphed by plotting the movement of a dynamic system such as a discussion of an issue or the creation of a project as it moves through time. Such a graph would produce a picture of the system as a whole, with each point on the graph representing the entire system at a particular point in time. As we follow the thinking as evidenced by the actions and verbalizations of the students involved in the discussion or project, we would see how that thinking revolved around one or more basins of attraction, its complexity limited only by the thinking of the participants involved. The more varied the attractor, the more complex the thinking.

The movement of a system through phase-space is driven by iteration through several levels of chaos. The first level is that of the fixed point attractor. In the classroom, students can make many decisions and solve many problems. Some of these decision and solutions require that the class come to consensus. Take, for example, the decision of where to go on a field trip. Brainstorming may involve putting forth several destinations, and the ensuing discussion will touch upon both positive and negative aspects of each proposed destination, but in the final analysis, a decision is reached about that particular field trip for that particular day. Movement around a fixed point, the destination for a field trip, is unpredictable in that some students will support one destination and others an alternate, but the group makes its decision and comes to rest at a fixed point.

The second level of chaos is that of the limit cycle attractor. In a classroom, students may debate the merits of a particular course of action, and find that there are at least two equally valid points of view. Because they are equally, or nearly so, valid, students find themselves attracted to one particular viewpoint, or basin of attraction, and thus the discussion cycles endlessly between the two basins. That is, they finally agree to disagree. Because of the robustness of the two basins, it can be argued that the second level of chaos produces stronger critical thinking, and indeed the authors have found this to be true. There are those who say that these two levels are not actually chaos, but are steps on the way to chaos. Others characterize the third level of chaos as "deep chaos." (Petree, p. 1)

The third level of chaos is reached through a series of bifurcation points, period doubling, or a catastrophe shelf. It is this level of chaos, deep chaos, that reaches the outer limits of the Mandelbrot set of complex numbers, the edge of chaos, where creativity and critical thinking are most in evidence. This is also the level where the brain reaches its highest level of functioning and the mind is at the optimum level for learning. When a system is stressed beyond a certain, unpredictable level, it disorganizes itself and then reorganizes into a new, more complex structure. It is at this level, that the strange attractor appears in such forms as the various and beautiful Julia sets.

Another principle of chaos theory that needs to be addressed here is the property of density. As movement in a chaotic system is traced through phase-space, it is seen to be very robust; that is, not easily perturbed globally even though locally there is variation. In a graph of a classroom discussion, there can be only one line showing the movement of the discussion around the basins, an apparently three-dimensional system. However, each person who participates in the discussion also has a "line" within the attractor. Each individual's "line" while close to the point that has been made, is not at exactly that point because of the individual's sensitive dependence on initial conditions, but it will be near that point because that is the point where the discussion is at that moment. Therefore, in an actual phase-space mapping of a classroom discussion of thirty students, there will be thirty lines, not one, showing the movement of the discussion with each line near each point but not exactly on it. However, globally the shape of the attractor is maintained whether you have one line for the system as a whole or thirty lines, and the property of density is evident.

Strange attractors can take many forms in any dynamic system. In education, a strange attractor can be an idea, a theory or hypothesis. It can be an approach to a solution; it can be an intelligence or learning style of the person involved in the learning process. It can be a discipline or subject content. But in looking at the creative, critical thinking dynamics in the classroom, it seems that true chaotic conditions must exist for critical thinking to take place.

This is in line with the current brain research that sees the brain and therefore the mind as a chaotic system. A theme that characterizes much of the research into the brain and its behavior as a system is that when the brain is in its optimum operating state, it is operating at the borderline between order and chaos, where systems are most creative and generative. Roger Penrose says that

> It would be my view that the brain in its conscious state (or the 'mind'?) is able to harness these effects and make use of whatever subtleties are involved at that delicate borderline between linear Schrodinger evolution and the apparent randomness of reduction, thereby achieving effects far beyond those attainable by the ordinary operations of algorithmic computers ... Any world in which minds can exist must be organized on principles far more subtle and beautifully controlled than those even of the magnificent physical laws that

have so far been uncovered. At least that is my own very strong opinion. (Hiley, p. 118)

Strange attractors, in keeping with their name, are different every time an event is graphed. A class may discuss the oil industry in social studies, and one basin of attraction may be the monetary contribution of the industry to humanity, with another basin being the harm done to the environment. The discussion and study may range from the money put into circulation by the hiring of employees, building facilities, to the rising cost of gasoline and its effect on our standard of living, to the environment destroyed by the processes of getting and refining the oil, to the advancement of scientific discovery through the use of petroleum products. Although two classes may discuss the same oil industry, the strange attractors can certainly be different, the basins of similar attractors can be different, and certainly the points of discussion will not only be unique to the class but to the individual; that is, chaotic in nature and unpredictable even by the best written lesson plans by the most competent teacher alive. While the global nature of the discussion (it will be about a particular aspect of the oil industry) and certain basins of attraction may be predictable, that is, globally stable, there will be, in the individual points/comments around these basins "infinite modes, infinite degrees of freedom, infinite dimensions." (Gleick, p. 137)

This idea of the strange attractor underlying seemingly random behavior was addressed as early as 1923, although chaotic dynamics was not understood at the time. Psychological type as a basis for behavior, if thought of in terms of a strange attractor, can be clearly seen as an underlying structure in classroom dynamics. That is, each psychological type becomes a feedback loop interacting with all other feedback loops, thus creating a strange attractor around an issue or a project. For example, all students in a classroom can be working on a single project, but if they are give the choice to compete the project in any form that they choose, psychological type as well as intelligence type would determine what the end product would look like. All projects would be about the same topic or issue, but all would be different in the approach to the issue and in the final presentation, even if all of them have the same outcome.

To further understand phase-space as it applies to the classroom, one needs to also understand the fractal nature of critical thinking. Critical thinking must have an attractor, must be about something. It is finite then by definition. But because it involves people who do it and the moment that it is done, it is also three dimensional; and, it is infinite in that it can be done about this something by an infinite number of people. It is then possible that an infinite amount of thinking can be done within a finite area. Thus we cite the definition that Gleick gives fractals: " … a way of seeing infinity." (Gleick, p. 98)

In mathematics, a classic fractal is the Koch snowflake in which an infinitely long line surrounds a finite area. If we look on the attractor as the original curve or equilibrium of a idea, and the breaks (fractals) on the curve as the thinking about the idea, then we can see a snowflake shape begin to emerge, its complexity limited only by the number of thoughts. The analogy holds true regardless of scale. One person can think an infinite number of thoughts about an idea through phase-space as easily as an infinite number of people can think an infinite number of thoughts about an idea through phase-space.

Summary

Thus we see that the universal principles of chaos hold true and apply to classroom dynamics.

> Simple systems give rise to complex behavior; complex systems give rise to simple behavior; and more importantly, the laws of complexity hold universally, caring not at all for the details of a system's constituent atoms. (Gleick, p. 304)

That is, complex systems, or creative, critical thinking can arise at any time, or cannot arise at any time during the learning process, but is recognizable as critical thinking if chaotic dynamics is understood by the teacher in the classroom. Chaotic dynamics in the classroom operate in concert with the brain, since both systems are nonlinear, rather than against the brain which can do actual physical damage.

Sensitive dependence on initial conditions determines many outcomes as does the push and pull of divergent ideas, and the fractal nature of critical and creative thinking creates often dramatic variety within a single moment. The presence of the strange attractor signifies structure, and defines true chaos as opposed to meaningless and random thinking, and helps the teacher facilitate creative and critical thinking in the classroom. And, finally, these principles hold true regardless of scale; that is, creative and critical thinking can be fostered for one student, a classroom or a school system through the application of the same principles of chaos.

CHAPTER 2

BRAIN-BASED TEACHING THEORY

More has been learned about how the brain goes about doing the many things that it does during the past decade than in all the years leading up to the 1990s. Much of this has been made possible because of new technology that has enabled researchers to look at the brain in action rather than after the fact. Because of this, a number of startling and not-so-startling discoveries have been made, and groups of educators have been taking new looks at classroom practices. This chapter outlines many of the new discoveries and their impact on the teaching/learning process.

There are several principles that current brain-based teaching research has uncovered. They are:

Each brain is unique.
Brains are globally stable but locally flexible, and are uniquely shaped by experiences.
Brains are incredibly complex and maintain their ability to restructure themselves throughout life.
Emotions are critical to the restructuring process.
Brains act to create meaning through a process of compare/ contrast and patterning.
Brains create meaning within contexts.

Each Brain Is Unique

Gerald Edelman, a Nobel Prize winning microbiologist-turned-neuroscientist told the *New York Times* that "The brain, in its workings, is a selective system, more like evolution itself than like computation." (Hooper, p. 62) This means that, unlike a computer, the brain restructures itself each time it experiences outside information. According to Michael Merzenich of the University of California at San Francisco, the global structure of the brain is set in early life and cannot be changed, but locally the structure is constantly changing through experiences and this continues throughout life. He found in a mapping study of numerous monkey brains, that each brain had a unique map, and that this map shifted when certain experiences were encountered. (Hooper, p. 61) Hooper goes on to assert "Your accumulated thoughts and actions weave your neurons into the unique tapestry of your mind." (Hooper, p. 63)

This uniqueness has been noted by numerous other researchers as a major principle of brain-based teaching research. Following a workshop facilitated by Randall Fielding, Dr. Jeffery A. Lackney noted that

> The brain is a vastly complex and adaptive system with hundreds of billions of neurons and interneurons that can generate an astronomical number of neural nets, or groups of neurons acting in concert, from which our daily experiences are constructed. Many findings seem obvious and intuitive, as one outsider asked me, "isn't all learning brain-based?" (Lackney, p. 2)

Much of Dr. Howard Gardner's research into multiple intelligences has focused on the different ways that children process information and has further strengthened the notion that we are indeed unique. His research has explored the many ways people learn, and established, at last counting, nine distinctly different ways. This research has had a profound effect on learning theory, and has led to new instructional design principles that take these intelligences into account. To summarize his theory, Gardner says that each of us possesses all nine intelligences, but that each of us has one prominent or dominant intelligence through which we tend to interpret the experiences we have. In a school classroom, experiences that tap into our dominant intelligence will result in a more comprehensive understanding of a concept.

Learning styles also contribute to the mix. Dr. Harvey Silver has detailed four learning styles that are characteristic of learning, and has linked these styles to each of the eight multiple intelligences. He says that each intelligence is focused in a different way in each of the learning styles, and that particular global characteristics of a learning style are fine-tuned with regard to the intelligence that is dominant for that individual. In other words, a person who is dominantly verbal/linguistic and whose learning style is mastery learning, will concentrate on journalism or technical writing, whereas the verbal/linguistic learner whose style is self-expressive will concentrate on creative writing such as poetry or playwriting. (Silver, 2000)

With each individual having a particular learning style operating within a particular combination of intelligences, it is easy to see that a common experience would, for each individual, excite a unique set of neurons and create a unique learning experience for that particular brain. Therefore, the process of learning at the outset can involve any one of a very large number of possible combinations of neural pathways. And, within the brain, prior experience having already restructured existing neural pathways, an entirely new restructuring takes place again. Thus, each learning experience is for each individual highly idiosyncratic and creates a unique structure within the brain itself.

Because each of us has a unique combination of the nine intelligences, the experiences we have, although they may be experiences common to many others such as those found in school classrooms, these experiences are processed uniquely, are categorized uniquely by each brain, responded to uniquely by each brain with the expected result that each brain is uniquely restructured in the process. Further, this restructuring will affect future restructuring thereby contributing to the "unique tapestry," in Hooper's words, that form the "me" of each human being.

Brains Are Globally Stable but Locally Flexible, Incredibly Complex, Are Uniquely Shaped by Experiences, and Maintain Their Ability to Restructure Themselves throughout Life

Early brain-based learning theories surmised that brains were largely fixed at birth and that the environment could make only minor changes in its structure. However, William Greenough of the University of Illinois., after extensive study of rat brains, concludes

> ... the brain is dynamic throughout life. The old view was that the neural architecture was fixed at birth or certainly at maturity. We saw the brain as static because we were looking at micrographs of dead tissue where nothing ever moves. Only in the last five years have neuroscientist become aware of the incredible structural plasticity of the brain. (Hooper, p. 66)

Lackney also notes that

> ... scientists used to think that the brain was hardwired at a very early age and set for the rest of life ... This assumption is only partially true today. Pruning does take place at an early age, but research has confirmed that nerves continue to grow throughout one's life ... This is a huge discovery and has implications for life-long learning. (p. 3)

In a keynote address to the Learning and the Brain conference in Cambridge, Mass., in 2002, Dr. John Ratey said

> We always have the ability to remodel our brains. To change the wiring in one skill you must engage in some activity that is unfamiliar, novel to you but related to that skill, because simply repeating the same activity only maintains already established connections ... The brain is amazingly plastic. In the past it was commonly accepted that any brain damage was permanent; once a brain region died, the function it controlled was gone forever. More than 500,000 Americans have strokes each year, killing many neurons and cutting many connections, yet in many of them, undamaged neurons take over, changing the number, variety and strength of the messages they send, rerouting traffic around the accident site. Rewiring is possible throughout life.

Lackney further says, as does Jensen, that an enriched environment can increase the number of dendritic connections which in turn increases the number of neural pathways a quanta of information can take to an increased number of categories which also increases the number of possibilities of connections between categories or schema. And all of this creates a heavier, more active brain. If the number of connections and the richness of the categories (or schema) created is directly proportional to the level of intelligence, as many think that it is, then an enriched environment also increases intelligence. Lackney says, "… the more enriched environment, the more enriched brain …" (p. 4)

Jensen explains it this way:

> The brain is designed to respond to stimuli by physically growing new, larger and more extensive dendritic branching. It also releases more enzymes, forms more glial cells (a form of brain "lubricant"), grows larger synapses (the connectors between cells) and gets heavier. Furthermore, this growth can happen *at any age* as long as the brain is stimulated properly. (Jensen, p. 62)

Thus it would seem that, while large or global structures are to a great extent fixed at some point in life, that interaction with the environment can and does alter the details of these structures. While pruning—the action of sloughing off unused or little used brain cells at periodic instances—may tend to fix in place certain structures, the brain can also, even while operating within those fixed structures, restructure the details to create an entirely new structure. It is the process of structure and restructure that forms the new dendritic connections to the existing categories (schema) that bends the fixed structures and creates the unique brain.

Emotions Are Critical to the Restructuring Process

Studies of endorphins have shown them to be important chemicals that regulate many of the functions of the brain. These are neurotransmitters that can alter and intensify a particular experience. Endorphins are the brain's pleasure chemicals and use some of the same receptors as opiates. In fact , the name *endorphin* is a combination of the words *endogenous* and *morphine* and is used to describe those natural opiates produced by our own bodies.

Lakney explains the process this way:

Brain research has confirmed that emotions are linked to learning by assisting us in recall of memories that are stored in our central nervous system. Emotions originate in the midbrain or what has been termed the limbic system and the neo-mammalian brain. Sensory information is relayed to the thalamus in the midbrain which acts as a relay station to the sensory cortex, auditory cortex, etc. When sensory information reaches the amygdale, another structure in the midbrain, that sensory information is evaluated as either a threat or not, creating the familiar fight or flight response—the physiological response of stress. This information is only then relayed to the frontal cortex, our higher cognitive functions, where we take the appropriate action.... (Lackney, p. 3)

Some researchers, according to Jensen think of the brain as a "box packed with emotions" (Jensen, p. 6) or as "a gland." (Jensen, p. 6). He explains that emotions are essential to learning in several ways. For example they can help us determine such things as wanting to learn about something or not, believing that the information is true or not, and how long to retain the information. He says, " Learners can understand a topic without having feelings about it, but it won't mean anything to them until a emotion is attached to it." (Jensen, p. 6)

Our feelings, says Jenson, can also become barriers to learning. "If our memories have strongly negative emotional content, they may activate inhibitory neurotransmitters" (Jensen, p. 8) thereby preventing connections from happening. Stress, likewise, can be both good and bad. Too much, and inhibitory neurotransmitters are released, and not enough doesn't keep the brain alert enough to recognize the experience. The brain requires novelty or anomaly to awaken curiosity and present a challenge. A stimulating environment, using ill-defined problems to solve, multifaceted approaches to a concept, diverse perspectives and variety can keep the positive neurotransmitters flowing and enhance the learning experience. On the other hand, threats such as humiliation for "wrong" answers, staying after school, teasing, sarcasm, ostracism, and tracking can create enormous amounts of stress and trigger the release of inhibitory neurotransmitters and prevent learning. Lackney explains that

Emotions aid in memory retention (learning) of this situation as being good or bad. Decreasing threat ("driving our fear", mistrust, anxiety and competition) through cooperation, providing safe places, and providing a motivational climate for positive emotions ensure that learning will be retained. (Lackney, p. 3)

The brain, he says, "learns best when confronted with a balance between stress and comfort: high challenge and low threat." (Lackney, p. 3)

It is clear, than, that emotions have more impact on learning than previously thought. By triggering the release of endorphins that reward the brain for meeting challenges, the emotions can optimize the learning experience, prepare the learner for novel learning experiences and can contribute to the growth of a larger, more complex, healthier brain.

Brains Act to Create Meaning through a Process of Compare/Contrast and Patterning

According to Globus, writing in response to David Bohm's body of work on Implicate Order theory, the mind creates meaning through a process of comparing possibilities with sensory input and determines where there is a fit. This is based on an *a priori* enfolding of all of the possibilities that exist within the universe. Rather than being what he terms as a "wet computer" or "biological instantiation of a universal Turning machine" (Hiley, p. 373), he thinks that "The holonomic system is initially full with all possible worlds; there is an *a priori* plenum of enfolded *possibilia* that is the fundamental reality." (Hiley, p. 373) He says

> The brain indiscriminately generates a holoworld of all possible worlds and, based on the match between the abstract specifications of its continuously-tuned holofilters on input and the abstract properties of the input flux, worlds are discriminately unfolded from the holoworld. (Hiley, p. 379)

In other words, the holoworld or schema, contains all the experiences, knowledge and information with attached emotions about a particular concept. When new information is encountered, the brain processes the information by performing a series of compare and contrast activities to decide where to attach this new information. It tends to put it where the best fits occur. For example, a child's schema about animals may contain a subset of information about dogs. Upon encountering a new dog, the child's brain helps the child decide whether or not to pat the dog by comparing the information about the new dog to information in the dog schema about dogs that are friendly and dogs that bite. The closest match to either the friendly or the biting group determines to a large extent the future behavior of the child towards the dog. However, if the dog in question matches the biting category but turns out to be friendly, the schema must be reorganized to accommodate this new information. The child has learned something new about dogs and animals in general.

At present, neuroscience is only beginning to grapple with the immensely intricate questions of how consciousness works. But what ever the specific mechanisms, it seems plausible to generalize that a great deal of conscious processing (including layers of the unconscious and perception) relies on some form of comparison and contrast activity. Memory, whether genetically acquired as instinct or experientially acquired as learning, lies at the root of the brain movement in which the mix of reason, emotion, brain states, perceptual regimes and immediate environmental influences unfold in conscious (explicate level) awareness as a stream of comparing and contrasting. These comparing and contrasting activities then refold into the background (implicate) levels of the brain to set the stage for further comparisons and contrasts. (Hiley, pp. 416–7)

In a study of dyslexia, fluency and the brain, Dr. Maryanne Wolf of Tufts University, in a paper presented at the Learning and the Brain conference in Cambridge, MA, in 2002, speaks of cell assemblies that behave as compare/contrast mechanisms for frequently perceived symbols or visual input. She said

... when an unknown visual stimulus is first detected by the retina, there is an activation in the visual cortex of multiple individual cells. These cells correspond to various features of the retinal image and are responsible for coding very specific types of information (e.g. horizontal, diagonal, curved lines, etc.). After multiple exposures to the same stimulus, the individual cells in the visual areas become a working unit, or cell assembly. These unified groups of neurons learn to work together in precise synchrony, so that recognition of frequently viewed stimuli (like letters) becomes so efficient, it is virtually "automatic." One result of these cell assemblies in the visual area is a reservoir of orthographic representations of practiced, frequently viewed letters, letter patterns and words.

Comparing and contrasting activities are interrelated with patterning. According to Lackney, (2002) the brain is happiest when it is able to create order out of random sensory receptions. He says that pattern making is a natural mechanism within the brain and that learning is optimized when information is seemingly random and disorganized and the learner is required to create order (or a pattern). He says, "The brain, when allowed to express its pattern-making behavior, creates coherency and meaning." (p. 3)

It is clear from these studies that the brain not only creates categories (schema, cell assemblies, compare/contrast patterns) through which it processes, stores and retrieves information, but also restructures through what Piaget described as an accommodation or assimilation activity these categories as it learns. Learning, therefore, produces changes not only in the physical structure of the brain but also in the intellectual structures of the mind.

Brains Create Meaning within Contexts

In an interview with Renee Weber of Rutgers University, David Bohm said, "I am interested in meaning because it is the essential feature of consciousness, because meaning is being as far as the brain is concerned." (Hiley, p. 436) He further explained

> There is no fixed meaning. That is its characteristic, that there is no final meaning. The whole point of meaning is that the content is in a context, which in turn is in a context,

and therefore meaning is not final. We are always discovering it, and that discovery of meaning is itself a part of the reality … when you say "I understand" you really say "I see the whole meaning of this." (Hiley, p. 441)

Heisenberg, in formulating his uncertainty principle, said that obtaining knowledge is never an objective process because it is biased by the method we use to obtain it. In other words, the context creates our understanding of the information we seek to understand. That is, whether the context is content-related, a social relationship, or a physical relationship, the context biases the information in some way, and this bias is unique to the learner because of *a priori* or previously learned information. This context-dependency can be useful to the learning process because of the brain's ability to reorganize its intellectual structures through assimilation or accommodation. Later retrieval is then realized more readily through recall of context as well as through recall of content.

"All learning," says Jensen, "is, in some way contextually embedded." (Jensen, p. 17)

He uses this information to advance the idea that novelty, which grasps the brain's attention and focus even though the concept is the same, can be achieved through the simple act of changing the physical environment. For example, having a class outside instead of at classroom tables, may help students remember the content better simply because of the change in location. He says that this gives the brain "more identifying clues for better retrieval." (Jensen, p. 17)

An experiment with rats in the 1960s showed that those rats raised in cages with lots of toys and who were handled by their caretakers had much thicker cerebral cortexes than rats raised in cages without toys and without being handled by their caretakers. (Hooper, p. 64)

It is well-known that feedback is an important contributor to the learning process. Recent studies have shown that feedback is most effective when it results from interaction with a context rather than from outside the context. That is, learning is most effective when brains are allowed time to reflect on "errors" rather than when information is presented as *a priori*. Indeed, feedback seems to be responsible for the emergence of human consciousness, according to many scientists. Penrose explains that feedback in the form of nuance from many sources has contributed to the survival of the brain as well as its development to a higher level than in other life forms. (Hiley, p. 118)

It is consciousness that enables the brain not only to learn but to be aware that it is learning and to be aware how and why it is learning.

Summary

Eric Jensen, on his website, wrote, "Brain based learning is the purposeful engagement of strategies based on neuroscience. (Jensen, www.jlcbrain.com)

Those strategies make use of the findings that every brain is uniquely shaped through many experiences, is complex, flexible, and capable of being restructured throughout life; that emotions are critical to learning; that meaning is created through a process of compare/contrast activities; and that meaning is created within contexts.

CHAPTER 3

FINDING THE STRANGE ATTRACTOR

The Structure Underlying Chaos

Research into critical thinking in classrooms from elementary school to graduate classes at universities has shown that whenever strong critical and creative thinking occurs, the dynamics of the classroom are chaotic. When critical thinking is a goal to ensure deep understanding of content, it becomes necessary to analyze classroom discussions, development of projects and other tasks with regard to the principles of the new nonlinear dynamic theory of learning. Specifically, if a strange attractor can be observed, then we know that iteration occurred. Iteration drives a nonlinear system, just as critical thinking is driven by such principles as reciprocity, empathy, and open-mindedness which equal iteration.

To find a strange attractor, classroom discussions and project activities must be graphed. It is possible to mentally graph a discussion, but that takes practice, graphing a number of discussions and projects, and a lot of experience in the implementation of the nonlinear dynamic learning theory. A phase-space graph, which is a visual depiction of the movement of a system through time and space, is three dimensional, and requires the xy axes as well as the z axis. To set up a graph, criteria must be established for each axis. For this purpose, let the basins of attraction lie along the y-axis, and let the x-axis be positive and negative. The third dimension of the graph, the z axis, and the element which ties it all together will be the line which connects the points on the graph and which denotes the time the point occurred. Thus each point (comment) must be numbered in the order in which it occurs as it is placed on the graph.

Graphing the Strange Attractor

It is easier to understand this graphing if we begin with a classroom discussion in which critical thinking is acknowledged to have taken place. Consider the following discussion that took place in a third grade classroom where nonlinearity and critical thinking both were commonplace.

It begins as the teacher sets up a discussion about the Exxon Valdez oil spill that had recently occurred.

Teacher: We're going to continue today talking about the oil industry, especially the Exxon-Valdez incident that we started talking about yesterday. One of the questions you had was why President Bush didn't go to Alaska to see for himself what had happened. Who has some thoughts about this?

- He could have had more important things to do.
- It was pretty important to the people there, and he could have gotten someone to do the other things like the vice president.
- He would have to sign his own name

Teacher: What was so important about the oil spill?

- Well, for one thing it killed a lot of wildlife.
- I saw the pictures on TV last night ... it was awful.
- Well, I don't like for animals to get hurt, but no people were hurt, and there are a lot of plane crashes that kill a lot of people.
- I think a lot of people were hurt. Look at the fishermen. Now they're going to be out of work.
- One man just bought a boat, and now he's going to lose it.

Teacher: Is there any way he can earn money now?

- Yeah, he can go to work for Exxon and clean up the sound.
- They're making a lot of money doing that.
- He can make more money in two weeks than he did all year fishing with his boat.

Teacher: Then, when the sound is clean, what can he do?

- See, that's the problem. The fish are all gone, and he doesn't have anything else to do. If he just knows how to do two things, clean up and fish, and they're both done, what can he do?
- Maybe he could catch something else. Lots of people catch seals in Alaska.

Teacher: What happened to the seals during the oil spill?

- I saw in the paper that they had to be washed off, and a lot of them died.
- They would have died anyway, because now they don't have anything to eat. The fish are all dead.
- He couldn't hunt either, because bears eat fish.
- They eat seals, too.
- Now, we don't have any fish to eat, and no gas to drive anywhere.
- There's lots more oil up there, and people can still make a lot of money with the oil companies there.
- If it wasn't for the oil companies, nobody would be making a lot of money in Alaska, because there isn't much else there but snow.
- If they keep spilling oil and killing everything, what will they do when the oil is gone?
- Then there won't be anything left up there at all.

Teacher: Is there anything that can be done before we end up with nothing in Alaska?

- They need to learn how to stop spilling the oil.
- We could get our oil from somewhere else.
- Well, we need the oil, but we don't need to destroy the land just to get it.
- And we shouldn't destroy anyone else's land either. Because if we do that just for our oil, they won't let us do it since they saw what we did to Alaska.
- Besides, they want the oil for their cars and stuff.
- Can we get the oil companies to think about that first before they start getting out the oil?

A reading of the transcript lets the observer see that the discussion revolves around three major points: "making money," "destruction of the environment," and "solutions to the problem." For the purposes of the phase-space graph, these points are called basins of attraction. That is, the comments in the discussion are connected either positively or negatively to one of the three major points. These basins can be placed at points along the y axis. "Making money" can be placed at one end of the y-axis, "destruction of the environment" can be placed at the other end of the y-axis, and "solutions" at about the center. Each comment that a student makes is placed at a point on the graph according to positive or negative feelings expressed about the central idea of the basins of attraction and according to whether or not they are very close or very far away from the central idea of the basins of attraction. This necessarily has to be arbitrary because of the interpretation of the researcher. This is not seen as a problem because it makes no real difference in the overall theory whether one person's graph is exactly like another person's graph of the same discussion because the basins of attraction and the movement around them still show up and the attractor can still be found.

Analyzing this discussion with regard to the principles of chaos theory shows that two of the principles nearly always work together: sensitive dependence on initial conditions and iteration. It can be seen that the students are looking at the event from at least two perspectives, that of the environment and that of the economy. They can be heard discussing these perspectives from both positive and negative viewpoints. For example, the view that no people were hurt elicits the comment that people were indeed hurt because many will be out of work. The comment that he can make a lot of money cleaning up the sound brings forth the view that even though that is true in the short run, in the long run he's still out of work. And this leads to considering possible solutions and concerns about the environment and economy. This is iteration at its best. In other words, a lot of good critical thinking was going on with the children realizing that there are lots of different points of view on a very real problem. Each student comes to the discussion from a singular perspective based on background, culture, knowledge and interest. (Sensitive dependence on initial conditions.). This perspective is broadened both individually and as a group (fractalness or self-similarity of scale) when these perspectives are considered and then used as the basis for forming a more informed idea of the problem (iteration), and as a basis for a solution of the problem. This calls on the students to generate ideas that perhaps have not been tried before, the creative/generative force of chaos. The principle of density is not addressed here because the overt comments are the only ones possible to transcribe. If, however, each student had written the comments that were being thought at the time the overt comments were made, density would be evident. It is enough to graph only the movement of the overt system through time/space to see the strange attractor.

This graph shows the discussion on a two-dimensional **xy** axis. The points have been numbered and labeled. (see Figure 3.1, p. 38) On this surface, it seems random and disconnected. However, when the third dimension, time, is added to the graph, the comments/points become connected, iterations are apparent, and the attractor appears with the three basins of attraction clearly delineated. (see Figure 3.2, p. 39)

The Didactic Lesson

Next, consider a typical teacher-directed third-grade lesson on the same topic. This lesson includes the introduction of the topic, the Exxon Valdez oil spill, the review, the objective, teacher input, guided practice, independent practice and closure. It begins with an introduction of the topic by the teacher.

Teacher: Today, students, we are going to talk about the oil spill in Alaska. Find the copy of the newspaper clipping about the incident that I gave you to read for homework last night. Yesterday we talked about how the oil industry had made life easier for the native Americans who live in Alaska, and had opened up many opportunities for people who wanted adventure and excitement in the far North. Today we're going to look at this tragic accident so we can see another side of the story.

- I brought in a picture of the tanker that was in the paper this morning.

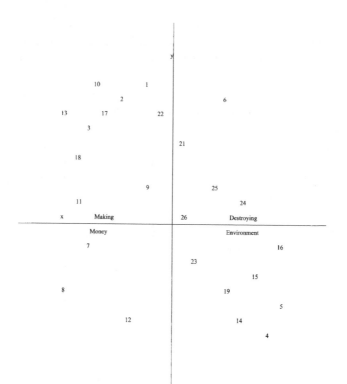

Figure 3.1   The two dimensional graph of a discussion where critical thinking was evident.

Teacher: Thank you. We'll add that to our bulletin board display so everyone can read it. Now, open your Social Studies books to the map of Alaska, and find Prince William Sound. Who can tell me the coordinates for Prince William Sound?

- On this map it's at B3.

Teacher: Good. Has everyone found it? Now, who can find Prudhoe Bay?

- It's at C1.

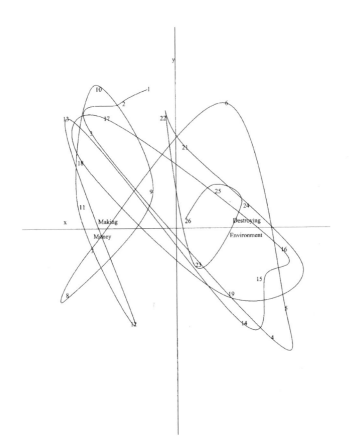

Figure 3.2   This phase-space graph using three dimensions clearly shows the strange attractor.

Teacher: Good. Does everyone see that? Now look at the world map on the wall and find Alaska. Darlene, can you come to the map and point to Prince William Sound on this map? Good. Thank you. Chris, would you tell the class what you learned from the newspaper article you read last night?

- It said that the captain of the tanker was drunk and let another man drive it, and he hit some sand.

Teacher: Anna, can you add to that?

- It said that about 11 million gallons spilled into the sound. And that a lot of animals have already died, and more are expected to die from the oil.

Teacher: What was the name of the ship, Mark?

- The Exxon Valdez.

Teacher: Who was the captain of the ship, Vanessa?

- Captain Hazelwood.

Teacher: Let's think about the consequences of the oil spill of the people in Alaska. Jacob, do you remember what one of the principal industries in Alaska is?

- Fishing, and catching King Crabs.

Teacher: How do you think the oil spill is going to affect the fishery workers and the fishermen? Jacob?

- When the fish and crabs die, they'll be out of work.

Teacher: Are fish and crabs the only animals that are dying? What do you think, Barbara?

- I didn't read it in this article, but on TV they said that the seals and water birds are dying, too.

Teacher: Do you remember when we talked about food chains in Science class? How plants are at the bottom of the food chain, and the larger and stronger animals feed on the smaller ones? That's why even though some birds and seals survive being coated with oil, they may die later, when their food supply is gone. They will either go somewhere else of die from starvation. The oil has killed many of the plants that are at the bottom of the food chain, so that even if the spill itself doesn't kill the animal right away the effects of the spill will affect the animals later. And that will mean people will be out of work because many jobs in Alaska depend on the sea and the animals that live there.

Is there another kind of business that will suffer because of the oil spill, John?

- The tourist industry will because nobody wants to see a beach covered with oil.

Teacher: Right, until the beaches and fishing and hunting areas are cleaned up, none of the people who go to Alaska for vacations will come. Those visitors spend a lot of money which provides a lot of jobs for Alaskans, such as hunting guides, people who run motes and hotels, restaurant workers, and people who have stores where tourists can buy things. All these people have been hurt by the spill, too.

I have some questions about the oil spill written on the chalkboard, and I would like you to use the article from the newspaper that you read last night as well as your Social Studies book to answer them. When you finish, put your paper, folded on the right hand corner of your desk and I'll come pick it up. Be sure to check it over before you hand it in. Your homework assignment is written on the board also. Copy it in your assignment book. Are there any questions? Okay, start on your questions now.

The questions on the board are:

1. *What was the name of the oil tanker?*
2. *Who was its captain?*
3. *How many gallons of oil were spilled?*
4. *What is the name of the sound where the oil spill occurred?*
5. *Name the major oil field in Alaska.*
6. *Using the map of Alaska in your social studies book, give the co-ordinates for*
   a. *Prudhoe Bay*
   b. *Prince William Sound*
   c. *Nome, Alaska*
   d. *Fairbanks, Alaska*
7. *Name three animals that have died as a result of the oil spill.*
8. *Name at least two kinds of jobs that have been lost because of the oil spill.*
9. *How long was the tanker that wrecked?*
10. *Who was driving the tanker at the time of the wreck?*

Homework: Write a paragraph explaining how the loss of fish in Prince William Sound will affect a waitress in a restaurant in Alaska.

An analysis of the discussion with regard to the principles of chaos theory shows that iteration does not occur. The students are responding to a set of questions offered by the teacher, and input comes from the newspaper article and the social studies book. There is no alternative viewpoint brought in other than a picture which is not made a part of the discussion. Sensitive dependence on initial conditions, therefore, is not a part of the dynamic. The critical thinking principles of considering alternative view points, reciprocity, and open-mindedness are not in evidence. Nor is the brain involved other than minimally. Students are asked to recall what they read in an article or to use skills taught at an earlier lesson about coordinates. They operate at the lowest level of Bloom's taxonomy. Any empathy they might have for the plight of the people and animals is reduced by the teacher to a clinical discussion of the food chain and the economy.

In attempting to graph this discussion, it becomes evident that there is only one perspective, only one basin of attraction, and therefore no movement on the y-axis. In addition, because there is no discussion of positive or negative aspects of that one perspective, there is also no movement on the x-axis. As a result, the third dimension of time cannot be added because it doesn't make a whole lot of difference when the individual points were made. They did not respond or correspond in any way to a previous point. Thus, the teacher-directed lesson graphs as a single very dense point. (see Figure 3.3, p. 43)

A Random Discussion

The next discussion, also took place in a third grade classroom. Here again the topic is the Exxon Valdez incident, and the teacher introduces the topic by referring to the newspaper article that was assigned for homework.

Teacher: Today we're going to talk about the oil spill in Alaska that I know has been on your minds. Find the newspaper clipping that I gave you to read last night so we can refer to it as we talk. Who can tell us what happened and where it happened?

- The captain of the boat was drunk and let someone else drive it and he ran aground.

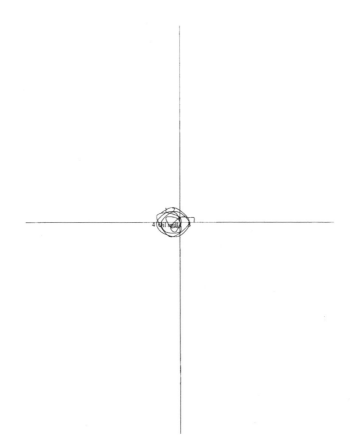

Figure 3.3   This graph shows that there was no critical thinking involved in this discussion.

- Over 11 million gallons of oil spilled out.

Teacher: Who remembers where this happened?

- It was Prince William Sound in Alaska. It killed a lot of animals like fish and seals and birds.
- I don't understand why they let the captain get drunk. They shouldn't let drunks be captains.
- Well, they didn't let him. They didn't know it. I think everyone on the tanker should have to know how to drive it.

Teacher: What is the biggest problem with the oil spill?

- How to clean it up. My mom said that Exxon should have to pay for all the clean up and pay a fine, too.
- My dad said that he wasn't going to buy any more gas from Exxon any more. He and Mom cut up their credit cards.
- That's not going to make any difference, nobody buys enough gas to make Exxon pay attention to it.

Teacher: The newspaper article mentioned that a group was on its way to help clean up the birds and try to save them. Why is this important?

- Well, birds are living things and we have to look after them.
- And they are part of the food chain.

Teacher: Right. Are there any other parts of the food chain that are being affected by the oil spill?

- Fish are, and so are crabs.
- I don't like crabs, so I don't think they're very important to the food chain. Besides we need gas more than we need fish.
- My mom said we get our fish from Japan and our gas from Saudi Arabia, so we don't need to get so upset about a little oil.
- I think it would be fun to work on a boat that gets crabs and lobsters.
- There was a movie last night on TV about a fisherman in Alaska who was about to lose his boat.
- Fishing is hard work and so is working in an oil field.
- That's why I'm going to college so I can work with my brain instead of my muscles.

Teacher: This certainly points up a problem that we seem to have everywhere—with drunk driving. And when the vehicle is a tanker with millions of gallons of oil, it's especially dangerous.

- I hope they put him in jail.
- My dad said they'll send him somewhere to dry out and then they'll put him in jail for a while.

- He'll be right back out on the street in a week. My uncle was caught driving drunk last week and even though it was the third time, he was out by the next morning.
- My mom drives drunk all the time, but they never catch her. She says that she drives real slow so no one will notice her.

Teacher: Do you think that stricter laws about drunkenness would have helped in the oil spill?

- Probably not. Who's going to know on a tanker in the middle of the ocean?

Teacher: How do you think the oil spill could have been prevented?

- Well, we could make all the drivers pass a test.
- They probably have to do that already.
- My dad says that they just hire anybody they can get because it's such dangerous work.
- I guess this wreck proves that!
- More fishermen get killed than they do on tankers, so I think that's more dangerous.
- There are a lot of dangerous jobs around, like being a policeman. You get shot at.
- You couldn't shoot a gun on a tanker—it would explode.
- I bet when those things explode they really go up like a whole lot of bombs!
- I saw a picture about an oil well fire that was worse. It was so hot it melted everything around it.
- Like that building that burned up last week. It was so hot that the steel rafters melted.
- I remember that. And they couldn't go near it until in the morning.

This discussion is entertaining, but an analysis shows that not only did critical thinking not occur, the entire discussion tends to dissolve into randomness. There is a new topic every sentence or two. Students are making independent comments rather than considering perspectives other than their own. They do not build on or add to the previous comment and do not remain on the issue. Most of their comments are pretty much off the wall. This discussion is impossible to graph because the points keep falling off the graph. There are no basins of attraction, no iteration, just a lot of initial conditions that never get iterated.

It is notable that critical thinking did not occur in either of the latter discussions, *and* there were no signs of chaotic dynamics. In the last example, randomness took over and the discussion wandered all over the place. In the teacher-directed lesson, the discussion was locked into a single, inflexible point with no possibility of movement.

Does this mean that whenever a chaotic discussion occurs that critical thinking will automatically take place? Yes, and no.

Globally, yes. A chaotic discussion involves iteration, using one idea to generate another one or to influence and change an old one. This consideration of perspectives is a part of critical thinking as is the generation of new ideas based on the thoughtful consideration of other ideas. And yes, because each idea brought to the discussion is personal; that is, sensitive to the initial conditions of the thinker. Yes, because it is fractal in that there are as many breaks (thoughts) on the curve of the perspective as there are thinkers about the perspective.

Locally, no. Just as there are quiet pools and fast moving streams side by side in a swift river, some students will fail to enter the flowing stream of the discussion, and after coming to a comfortable point will remain there undisturbed by the controversy around them. One may at some point join the discussion, or may not, and it is not possible to predict which students will opt out of the flow or at what point. This is simply a factor of the universal principal of chaos that says that simple systems may give rise to complex systems, and they may not. And complex systems may give rise to simple systems, and they may not.

Does this mean that unless a discussion or classroom setting is chaotic, critical thinking will not take place? Here again the answer is yes and no. It is remotely possible for critical thinking to occur at any time under any circumstances, but is very hard for students to do it without encouragement. Most young children do not think critically in school for many reasons. (Davis-Seaver, 2001) And in situations such as the teacher directed lesson or the random discussion, they are highly unlikely to do so.

If, then, it is true that a basic purpose of our schools is to show students how to be good critical and creative thinkers, and to encourage them in this crucial undertaking, should we not put them in an environment that is most likely to produce critical and creative thinking? Such an optimal learning environment would be nonlinear, would actively involve the brains of the students such that neural pathways would be strengthened and new ones created, and comprehensive understanding about content would be most likely to occur. This is the environment advocated by the nonlinear dynamic theory of learning.

Summary

Finding the strange attractor requires graphing student comments and discussions on a phase-space graph. After much experience with graphing, it can be done mentally, but until then it is best to transcribe and graph the discussion or project development in order to see the attractor. In-depth learning of content requires critical thinking about content, and when this occurs it will be evidenced through the appearance of the strange attractor on a phase-space graph. While critical thinking on the part of an individual student cannot be predicted, a nonlinear environment makes it more likely that this will happen.

CHAPTER 4

HEADFIRST AND ON PURPOSE

Over the Catastrophe Shelf

The purpose of university level classes as well as those in elementary school is to bring about a deeper understanding of the concepts, issues and ideas that drive the content of any class. Having students engaged in topics that will bring about such depth of understanding is crucial to this underlying purpose, and therefore a way of causing this to happen is also crucial. The former requires action on the part of the students, but the latter lies in the domain of the teacher. And it was in this domain that the authors began to address the importance of chaotic dynamics within a classroom to create critical/creative thinking and the attendant challenge of bringing this dynamic into being. This experiment called on the basic principles of chaos theory: sensitive dependence on initial conditions, iteration, fractalness, and the presence of a strange attractor. Other principles considered were those of the irreversibility of time, the catastrophe shelf and the three levels of chaos.

In an educational paradigm, creating a catastrophe shelf (also known as a bifurcation point) that would enable students to move from the known with its certainties and predictable right answers to the unknown wherein they would construct their own belief system and knowledge about an issue was the task not only for the students, but also for the instructors

While the three levels of Chaos can be graphed in phase space, it is the third level that produces the wild and turbulent strange attractors, and it is this level that results in deeply creative/critical thinking and activities, that bonds its participants into their own universe.

It was to this level the authors sought to bring students in a conscious and deliberate way in order to generate a depth of understanding of the content of the course in a way that was new to all participants.

Simply expecting students to think creatively, critically and in depth, however is not realistic since the thrust of many high school curricula is passing tests for which critical thinking is neither desired nor encouraged. Therefore, it was necessary to initiate a process through which students would think critically and creatively at the same time they were learning content. After experimenting with setting up dynamics that produced level one chaos, and level two chaos, the authors searched for the most creative and generative level of chaos, the third level. In order to do this, catastrophe shelves were created at which time the students were figuratively pushed over it— or it was arranged for them to do it themselves.

Three different classes were used for this research. One was an undergraduate class in *Psychological and Sociological Foundations of Education*, a second one was a graduate class in *Children's Literature*, and the third was a *Theory of American Education* graduate class.

The First Class

To institute the changes in the undergraduate *Psychological and Sociological Foundations of Education* class, the instructor first defined for the students an activity that consisted of a portfolio which was to include a summary and analysis of each chapter of the textbook to be considered during each class session. This summary/analysis would be due at the beginning of each class session and would act as a "ticket" to enter the class. At the beginning of the process, Socratic questioning was initiated by the instructor to elicit critical thinking from the students. Eventually, the students were able to engage in a Socratic discussion as the instructor literally backed out of the discussion and allowed them to take over the responsibility of the inquiry.

The instructor restructured the class so that students would focus on issues, and the analysis of issues, rather than on memorizing dates and events, and apply their understanding to current events and issues. Instead of the traditional lecture-note taking method, the class was redesigned to empower students, giving them the responsibility for their own learning.

The class was structured around the following activities:

Chapter analysis: Students were required to analyze each chapter and bring that summary to class as an admission ticket to class. Attendance was taken by checking each summary. This process ensured that each student in attendance had a common basis for discussion.

Field Activities: Students were required to attend and critically analyze five field activities; attending school board meetings, PTA, social activities, interview teachers, students or parents and so forth, or any activity relating to public education.

Portfolios: Students were required to maintain portfolios containing approved chapter analysis, analysis of field experiences, two examinations, and any other materials that they felt would demonstrate their understanding of the issues being discussed. The portfolios would be graded at the end of semester, but at any time that a student wanted to know his/her grade, he/she had the option of requesting that the instructor grade the portfolio using grading established at the beginning of the class.

Initially, the instructor found it necessary to lead the discussions and direct the interactions among the students, but using a Socratic discussion format. Students tended to answer only questions posed by the instructor, and would look for confirmation that their response was correct. If they wanted to speak, they raised their hands.

However, as the class progressed through the semester, students no longer asked permission to speak nor did they look for confirmation that they were responding correctly. One day the instructor was late for class, and on arrival discovered that the students had started their discussion on Funding for Public Education without waiting for the instructor to start the discussion. Students were pointing out the inequality in funding for education, how education would be never be equal with the present funding procedure, that there is no constitutional provision for education and therefore inequalities in education challenged in the courts would be decided on a case-by-case basis, that states would always have problems with a constitutional amendment providing for education.

In this culturally diverse class, students initially analyzed issues only as they related to their culture, ignoring the impact these issues had on other cultures. As the class progressed, however, each cultural group moved out of the parameters of their culture as they discussed issues. They moved toward solutions to problems that were neither cultural nor experience bound, but instead were common to the group. In most classes, female students were more conversational than males. In this restructured class, for some reason, males became equal participants.

The Second Class

In the second class, *Children's Literature* graduate class, the instructor restructured the all-lecture format to that of brief lecture at the end of the class, and, at the beginning, small discussion groups which led to reports on their discussions to the whole group which in turn led to Socratic discussions around issues of reading, trade books, and literacy. Class time was focused on in-depth discussions of a large number of trade books, exploring the reading, writing, literature connections, and attending literacy events in the community such as storytelling events and children's theater productions.

The 42 students were asked to organize themselves into groups of four or five. Each group was given a selection of books to read together. Their assignment was to read as many of the books in their group as possible. Then they were to select one book that appealed to them, was particularly significant for whatever reason, and to choose a member of the group to present it to the class with a synopsis of their discussion about it.

For the first session, 30 minutes were allotted for the reading and discussion in the small group and another 30 minutes for the large group discussion, after which the instructor planned to lecture briefly on the first genre of children's literature.

During this first session, after some few minutes organizing themselves into groups the students spent about 40 minutes reading and discussing all the books. The presentations of each group to the class took about 10 minutes, averaging about 1 and a half minutes per group. Very little about their discussion was included. During the lecture, the instructor included some of the comments that were overheard during the small group discussions. In addition students were asked to contribute to the lecture by discussing a particular book that they read in their group that was an example of a point being made. After this first class, many students remarked to each other and to the instructor that they enjoyed the chance to actually read the books— many of them had never read them even though they were considered classics and "must reads" for elementary school students. They said that during their elementary years, all they read were basal readers, and homework left them little time for any other reading. Several of the students lingered awhile to finish up a book they had started but didn't finish, or to quickly scan a book they didn't get to see.

During the second class session, grouping took less time, and reading got underway quickly. There also was more discussion and the presentations took much longer. Students began to write down titles and authors, and wanted the books passed around. However, their years of training in passive to no interaction with the instructor led to there being little participation during the lecture except when asked. At the end of class, there was more passing around of books and writing down of titles and authors and students lingered in the classroom. The instructor told the students who were staying to continue their discussion to cut off the lights as they left.

During the third class period, lively discussions of the books took place, students were reading portions of them to each other, and the decision of which book to present to the class began to take longer. Several groups asked to present two books instead of just one. Presentations were more in-depth, and students began to voice their own opinions about the underlying themes and purposes of the books and to report alternative opinions within the group. They read aloud portions of the books to the class to underscore their points. During the instructor's lecture portion of the class, students began raising their hands to interject points and to show books that illustrated points. It was evident that they had read the textbook as well as the trade books.

The fourth class period was a study of poetry, and it was here that the class actually became a learning community. None of them was familiar with more than a few poems, and there was universal reluctance to read children's poetry books. However, they dutifully grouped themselves. Instead of the instructor handing out the books, students delegated a member of each group to choose a selection of books, and they began to read. The instructor asked students to look for examples of specific elements of poetry rather than simply read and present, but to read the books first for enjoyment. Comments such as "Here's a neat poem, read this one next" and "Listen to this" were heard as students moved from reading silently alone to sharing with their group. Groups began to read to each other, and some students as they overheard conversations, walked over to visit with another group and then to share with that group what they had read. As they began to find examples of such elements as rhythm that carries part of the message of the poem, rhyme that enhances meaning, figurative language, simile, metaphor, onomatopoeia, and to separate ballads from lyrical poems, limericks from epics, the conversation within and among groups increased. Their presentations were very animated. Students were not asked to present the elements that they found, but instead to follow the usual procedure of presenting a book that the group found significant for whatever reason. The presenters read entire poems, and several times other members of the same group would present poems that they individually found meaningful or interesting or just fun to read. For a while it looked like they were going to read just about every book aloud to the class. The instructor began the lecture with a discussion of the elements of poetry that students had been asked to find examples of, and as the instructor would finish an explanation of the element, students were not waiting to be asked to give examples. Hands would go up and they would read what they had found. Soon they were not raising their hands, but instead would say, "Here's a good example of that," and would stand and read the poem or the part that applied. In this way, students took over the class entirely. They read all the examples of one element, and when they finished instead of waiting for the instructor to resume the lecture, the students moved to the next element on their list. The class moved closer together, and small conversations about individual examples of poetic elements would erupt, then subside, as another speaker would take the floor. Comments such as "I thought that was what it was!" or "When you read the poem aloud you can really feel the beat—it makes a difference in how well you understand the poem."

A student, in speaking to the whole class, said that she had always disliked poetry because in elementary school it had always been made such a chore. They had to figure out the rhyme scheme (abba and such) and weren't allowed to interpret it but had to accept what the teacher read from the manual. There wasn't much reading or writing poetry just because you wanted to or because you had something to express. When the instructor asked her how she felt about poetry now, she said that she enjoyed this class about poetry, and that if she had been able to study it in discussion groups in elementary school, she probably would like it.

Then began a discussion on methods of teaching poetry in elementary school not led by the instructor but instead by the students. Everyone had a story to tell, and the consensus was that children's poetry is fun, interesting, and has much to offer if students are allowed to enjoy it, to discuss it, and to share their opinions, interpretations and understanding with each other without interference from a teacher armed with a teacher's manual and a test at the end of the unit.

At the end of the class, which ended late, students hung around finishing discussions, trading books, asking to borrow one or two books for a couple of days, writing down more titles and authors. Students were sharing their notes with each other; current teachers were talking about how they could use poetry in their classes.

One of the projects in this class was to develop a whole language lesson plan from one of the books they had read or included in their book files. After several lessons such as that on poetry, they began writing these plans, and the creativity being generated in class though their reading and discussion had positively affected them. Plans included a broader range of disciplines and literature genre. They were combining narrative with poetry, poetry with informational literature, biography with science and math, narrative as a way of introducing or expanding social studies issues and topics.

Methods of teaching included a variety of activities, especially student-directed ones, story maps, writing, creating books, plays, songs, and art. Learning centers used books as themes under which students could derive math, science, and social studies activities. The planning was broad, more in-depth, and comprehensive. They openly worked with each other and supported each other. Two students used the same book, but developed lesson plans on different grade levels. They were surprised at the insights this activity on their part gave them about the teaching/learning process.

It became clear to everyone in the class that something very unique and very moving had occurred. In spite of the large size of the class, the students experienced a closeness and a supportive environment not usually found in graduate classes. Their creativity was evident in every project, and was received with enthusiasm by their fellow class-mates. Issues of teaching and learning were at the core of their dis-cussions rather than lists of books or grades. They were expanding their knowledge of children's literature not as an end in itself, but as an important part of the larger picture of meaningful learning in the elementary school. They took over the class in a purposeful and thoughtful way, including the instructor as part of their community while taking responsibility for their own learning, and never hesitat-ing to jump into the lesson at any point. Groups became more fluid, with many students forming new associations. Discussions were live-lier and presentations more in-depth. Opinions and examples abounded, both from books that were present, books remembered, and personal experience. Classes always ended late.

The Third Class

In the third class, the *Theory of American Education* graduate class, the instructor also asked his students to compile a portfolio consist-ing of "seed" papers, "I search" papers, and summary/analyses of two textbooks. The class was focused for the entire semester on the sin-gle topic "What Is Education?" considering a different aspect of this topic during each class session. Students were asked to change para-digms with regard to specific examples and issues, and to explore the implications of these changes. Again, a Socratic discussion format was used, rather than lecture. The instructor also instituted a discus-sion forum on a Web Page to which the students, as well as interested faculty, were invited to contribute.

In this class the catastrophe shelves were more obviously arranged by the instructor. The first catastrophe shelf was the decision for or against engagement: a two-variable shelf that needed to be hurdled before the students could get beyond a three-, four- or eight-variable shelf that would thrust them into a parallel universe of third-level chaotic discourse. To reach this goal, students began with a whole group discussion on the topic, *What is education?* This became a level one chaotic discussion as more and more students generated ideas and made efforts to move toward consensus about it.

Here is part of the discussion from the first level of discourse. In answer to the question, What is Education? The responses were:

survival
life experiences
enlightenment
understanding
excitement
giving
learning
thinking
information
sentences
getting along with others
caring
teaching
violence
facilitating
counseling
troubles
encouragement
drugs
listening
knowledge
guiding
expressions
emancipation
patience
balloons
noise
confusion

schools
identity
home
teachers
peers
drugs
freedom
books
community
anxiety
village
politics
children
money
technology
parents
capitalism
socialism
promissory notes
conferences
diversity
registrars office
financial aid office
individuals
long lines
understanding yourself
expectations
cultures
chairs
dictation
geriatrics
language
teamwork
friends
solitude
communications
innovations

creativity
homework
corporal punishment
oh yeah
love
social work
pain
ethics
paddles
what was the last one
do you disagree with anyone
do you disagree with paddles
paddles
can you give me an example
well you are around corporal punishment you know I was around corporal punishment and I got my share of whacks so
can you give me an example
of a paddle? sure
of maybe 12 inch 18 inch in length swung at a high velocity
class
communications
chuck taylor
uniforms
social economic classrooms
human resources
lockers
slavery
servitude
pimples
dedication
buses
socialization
disciplinary letters
indoctrination
letter of warning from the dean
well we know he gets paddled and letters
chaos

unexplained tardies
classroom management
can someone give me an example of classroom management
discipline
set of rules to follow
different levels
Saturday detention
consequences for your actions
changing gears
priest
patriotism
reward
enrich
federalize
snakes
liberation
broad mind
propaganda
aggression
laboratory fires
jargon
class clown
exactly
ignorant
hey, careful now
maturity
clubs
band
glee club
media
intelligence
p. a. announcements
dialogue
personalities
progress reports
assessments
corrals

vegetables
surfers
sororities
class trips
back of the bus
music
alcohol
oh my
dating
rosa parks
brown
versus
num chucks
puritans
parking lots
competition
overdue
prejudice
kiss
graduation day
kkk
little children
society
brown v board of education
plessy v ferguson
peer pressure
jim crow
jim crow laws
busing
desegregation
segregation
back to school sales
theater
Satan
science and math
curriculum
government

mass destruction
tolerance
grammar
hell
bake sales
science
walk a thon
personal growth
diabetes
tendinitis
second hand smoking
multicultural

Although this discussion seemed random, the focus and direction for the students was to try to come up with a single good definition of what education is. Many of the comments dealt with superficial issues, simply saying the first thing that came to mind. None of the participants in the discussion left their initial conditions, and very little iteration took place. That is, they were not listening to each other to improve old thoughts or to generate new ones. They were simply skimming the surface of whatever comes to mind.

To approach the next catastrophe shelf, the students were asked to pair up and create a dichotomy growing out of the whole group discussion. Each one would pick an aspect of the discussion that resonated, and discuss it with another person who had a different point of view. Now the task was not consensus but instead a discussion that involved two different but equally valid perceptions of the basic question, **What is education?** Because both viewpoints were equally valid, the conversation cycled between the two, never coming to rest at one point or the other. It was a level two, damped and driven chaotic system. What follows is part of this discussion.

Group 1
—Our dyad talked about teaching and facilitating. For teaching we said teaching is person facilitating.... the thoughts and opinions of me with uniform, conformity, and coercion as the aim. Conforming is the result and it begins and ends with one thing.
Instructor—Do you agree with that?

—Ah yes.... and opposed to that is facilitating. We choose to allow one to grow at one's own pace with unlimited restraints and allow one to reach his own personal goal and it continues anywhere, anytime, any place for a lifelong time.

Instructor—*Okay, thanks ...*

—We choose caring and violence and under caring we said it was always a plus, it can go along way, it changes things, it shows love, it can motivate, it can change violent attitudes, it can help others to be helpful. Under violence.... it has no merits, its senseless, its a goal of ignorance, its depressing, it means no good, it leads to no good ends, it also results in injury, it hurts everyone.

—To summarize under caring we came to the conclusion that it can change a multitude of things.... and under violence we said it was just bad.

Instructor—*Just bad ... okay, do you agree with that?*

—yes

Instructor—*do you have anything to add?*

(shakes head no)

Instructor—*Okay. Next group.*

—We choose love and pain and under love we stated that it created a degree of success and approvement and it was shown by example in both giving and receiving, it makes one acceptable and happy over all.... and under pain ...

—We said it that can be used as a form of discipline by teaching as a lesson so to speak, that it creates caution as well as suppressing future actions, it maybe is done to receive the initial pain ... it allows you to learn from your mistakes ... and it can evoke new emotions for pain that were not previously experienced for pain ... for example irritation, hate ... it still shows emotional growth.

Instructor—*thank you.*

—We choose encouragement ... it fosters growth, education, and success in life ... it (makes) achievers, you're challenged, you become a risk-taker, and performer.

—I said in media ... more information available ... it brings the world as a lot closer to you, its an opportunity to broaden the information you receive in as a hurry.... hear other opinions ... recorded history ... international.... provides first hand knowledge of the world wide important information ... provides as a check of what is happening in the world.

Instructor—thank you.

—We did Competition and Teamwork.... under competition we said strive to be the best number one, think independently allowing yourself to do your own work, learn more on your own, its good for capitalism and an economy to keep costs down, increase productivity, ensures progress because you don't want to rely on what's been, teaches survival skills and can have some excitement.

—For teamwork we said two heads are better than one, more intelligence in as a group, to share, learn co-dependency to a certain degree, learn how to compromise pursue the same goals, develop your skills of communication, promotes diversity, ensures a sense of community at least within that team and in a broader sense of community, get continual feedback from the teamwork, promotes self-esteem from the positive feedback, and allows you to stay on-task.

Instructor—thank you. Do you agree with that?

—yes

Instructor—anything to add?

—Well, competition leads one to think that the best is never good enough.

—For teamwork, it allows for group support and feedback, provides as a check and balance system, and theoretically no one is left behind if all parts are working together for the best possible outcome.

Instructor—Alright thank you, thank you.

—We had classroom management and listening. In order for teachers to maintain good classroom management, teachers/facilitators must first respect their students or audience and respect for their students or audience, support from other staff members such as teachers, co-workers, and administrative staff, and support from parents, consistency with all goals and ability to plan well will enhance one s exhibiting and retaining good management skills.

—Listening involves attention of students in understanding, awareness, and respect for themselves as well as their teacher and fellow classmates. Listening means be able to interpret and focus on what is being presented, it is considered doing the right thing.

Headfirst and on Purpose

Having fallen over the decision shelf of engagement in the issue, what seemed like a simple question now looked very complex. Students had now reached the critical shelf, and it was time for them to throw themselves over, headfirst and on purpose.

For this multi-variable shelf, a question was posed to which there is no answer and to which the answers are infinite: *What is education?* Upon returning to the whole group discussion format, it was clear that students were iterating the previous discussions among themselves, creating their own variables, and with the posing of the question again, plunged headlong over the shelf.

Students began to question not only the historical definitions of education, but to question the question itself. Is education something that is out there or is it an unlimited process that recognizes no parameters, having no beginning and no end. If there is no beginning, where do we start or is there no start just an *is being*? Out of this encounter were generated anomalies, questions, paradoxes, metaphors and similes. In the search for clarity of meaning, a new creation came into being—their understanding of the philosophical issues and foundations of education in a way that they had never encountered before. They left the class changed in fundamental ways, educated. Thus the irreversibility of time took effect, they could never again be like they were before the discussion. From a paradigm of simplicity and superficial understanding of the content of the class, they were now in a paradigm characterized by complexity and depth of understanding. They were making the unknown known, and in the process began to create other areas of unknowing into which they could venture with confidence. Here is the level three discussion, again addressing the topic *What is education?*:

—Survival
Instructor—Can you explain that further, can you embellish that?
—To gain the knowledge necessary to survive at whatever level, economic level that you care to participate in.
—To sustain life.
Instructor—Can you embellish that or explain what you mean.

—*You learn and you try to figure out ways to exist on this planet.*
Instructor—*B, do you agree with that?*
—*Education is expanding your knowledge ... to live both socially, economically.*
—*How about education is to keep out ignorance.*
Instructor—*Can you give an example of that?*
—*Sure, somebody tells you something that was told to you that is true but we really don't know that so we take it as blind faith. Quite frankly that could be our ignorance for not disproving or proving it.*
Instructor—*T, do you agree with that?*
—*Not necessarily proving it but maybe going along with what is actual what is evidence and then through trial and error.... but some things are just known that are truth that are sometimes based on cultural ... um economic, philosophy ... what have you.*
—*The question is what is education?*
—*I would have to agree with what B said ... that education is learning and being able to apply what you've learned to your daily life. Learning is change so I believe that education is change whether it's positive or negative you can learn some negative things you can learn positive things. I think education is more of what you've learned and applying what people learn.*
Instructor—*Does anyone disagree with her?*
—*I don't disagree but I have a question. We all have an idea of what education is based on ... as B said, everything around us, but can't you also say that education is an abstract concept and it can't be defined any way than with other abstract concepts so there's no way to define it—education.*
Instructor—*Does anybody disagree with her?*
—*Yeah, I do. I think the definition of education is defined as one that has been given to us even if education really doesn't exist.*
—*I'm not saying it doesn't exist but I'm just saying that it is an abstract concept.*
—*No, I'm saying that education doesn't exist, I think learning exists but education doesn't exist. Education is a label that was forced at us that we took without we being able to prove it. Therefore, in my opinion, education doesn't exist. But learning exists.*
—*Well then, what is learning?*

—*The assimilation of anything new that was not known before.*

—*Or may I add to that, anything not distributed by those who wish to provide someone a controlled environment so that they may cater to the behavior that is expected of them. In other words, I would agree that education itself is just a norm or a concept within a particular area ... a concept to provide a means of maintaining one's position—a function.*

—*Well see, I don't think that is learning. I think that is discipline.*

—*That is discipline in essence but not discipline of what is going to be performed in that particular environment. Therefore in order to maintain the attention span.*

—*Learning doesn't take place in controlled situations and that is not the case as learning will take place greater in an uncontrolled situation than it will in a controlled situation. Therefore that is just a matter of discipline and in discipline somebody will teach you something new and that is just a meager and outmoded form of teaching. But that is not education and that is not learning.*

—*Well I have to agree and disagree on that with you because in a controlled environment it is based on the criteria and the level of the criticism of that particular thing in the learning environment. It's based on what is being contributed, on what is being allowed into that environment.*

—*I don't think that education always happens in as a classroom setting or in a controlled situation. You get education just walking down the street.*

—*Is that education or is that learning?*

—*I feel like that is education because I am learning things that contribute to my education which contributes to learning to deal with life ... learning to handle life.*

—*So what you are saying is that learning is because you know more.*

—*Well, yes but it doesn't have to be know more in textbook knowledge.*

—*Well, what if you just know more and I heard a poem once that said the more you know the more you forget the more you forget the dumber you are so don't know anything.*

—*Okay, let's just say that education is the overall process of learning of whatever it is of whatever could be there. It's just the overall process of learning because education I believe begins in the home. Because, think of a little baby that starts to cry and knows that they can get their parents attention. You know once that child learns that they can get their parents attention just by crying then sometimes they'll do that. So education is the overall total process of learning throughout life.*

—So you're saying that education is in fact learning and learning is in fact education. They're one and the same.

—No you can learn more ... when the child cries and he sees a response from somebody ... but then that somebody is there ... the role the parents play in education is by not coming. Sometimes you don't always get what you want. When that child cries he is not going to get as upset ... teaching is education but to teach somebody you can't just teach nobody.

—That's right because if you have teaching you have learning but where is the education?

—The relays between the two.

—There's only two parts of education? The word education is just a fictitious label that somebody has put down in the dictionary that we accept as the major umbrella for everything that takes place with knowledge.

—You can't take a word in the dictionary because.

—Well that's right. So education really may not even exist.

—Wouldn't that be the body of knowledge in a class to learn?

—I don't know.

—It's life experience, trial and error.

—Well, can't we look at it as education is the step of your either the receiver or you are the ...

—Deliverer ?

—Yes, it depends on the amount of knowledge being used. So learning causes the educational process and there's also the learning process in the leadership ability of the discipline but never-the-less it continues ... that's the way I look at it. I'm trying to look at it in the military sense as the foundation of research. That's the controlled environment and in an uncontrolled environment that is what is being brought in is being rejected in reference to ...

—I'm sorry what did you say about being rejected?

—Yeah, whatever is being brought in is being rejected

—Is that uncontrolled?

—Anything that is being brought into an environment is being controlled or uncontrolled environment based on whose in bringing it in but at the apex or should I say the center of the environment or the wheel or who is delivering the data or the learning process that is a case you can

continue but if something comes in that is not acceptable as to maintain that the A and B and C has a relationship there, that is rejected. It has no means of being maintained.

—Okay, so we're talking about essentialism but that hasn't settled the question. The question is whether or not people learn … in what context.

—I can't in what is not acceptable to him, I can't learn …

—No what I am saying is that in most cases you can look at … okay you can look at who is providing the educational concept. The learning ability, the learning ability depends on the attention span, on what is being shared, but what is also being left out of it. If you bring something in that is not a part of the curriculum then it is not a part of the relationship of A and B and C and the C is being rejected…. it doesn't fit … I'm not saying that you don't have the ability to learn but you are being controlled in learning. Now if you bring it in I will say yes, this is how it works and this is what we are talking about and therefore it is now an uncontrolled situation.

—So what you saying then is that a person can't go out of his house, educate themselves, and learn something new, unless somebody else delivers it to them?

—Everything is delivered in the sense in which it is being received so it has nothing to do with your again quote your abilities unquote but looking at you as an individual …

—That tree is not providing a person but I can learn a great deal from that tree out there.

—But the tree doesn't have to be a person.

—But you said the person has to deliver to you.

—The object is now a person or a thing it could contribute to your learning ability provided that you provide a reference of what it is your looking at therefore the tree is educational but yet you will learn more of that tree by examining it by taking it apart, feeling it, touching it, that is the learning concept and yet education continues.

—So your saying that it is educational.

—Everything is educational but what is the level of it being brought into the universe…. is it an controlled environment or is it an uncontrolled environment where everything comes in to serve a purpose … its a process. The question is, are you able to learn what is almost always provided.

— Then tell me when education is there and when learning is not taking place.

— Ah …

— You said almost always so there must be a place in which education is taking place and learning doesn't.

— In the senses, the sensory concept.

Learning is still there.

— Yeah, but the things is that we're leaning towards communication between one person and another … by being aware the knowledge of something is different … what education is. It continues the learning process because it depends on how you are being able to receive it. Do you use it, does it have a function, what purpose does it serve?

— Okay, I still didn't hear if education takes place and learning is not taking place.

— To learn to read you have to be open to the experience. They can teach you all day long but.

— That's not the point. The question is does education take place when there is no learning.… when there is no learning does education take place.

— Yes, you see that you can deal with generalizations …

— You're still learning.

— No it is new.

— It doesn't have to be new to learn.

— No, it is new whatever new is.… as long as you are aware with your senses to pick up that something is now different … so therefore that difference is new.

— Yes, but education continues because it doesn't stop there.

— Sittin' here I didn't follow everything but it sounds like you just said two different things.

— Yes, I did.

Several differences in this discussion are readily apparent. One is in the role of the teacher, and the participation. After the initial phase of getting the discussion started and a few gentle nudges back to the central question, the teacher backed out of the discussion and let the students take over. Instead of simply saying one or two words that came to mind as in the first consideration of the topic, now the students had a lot to say about it, in much broader terms, and a wider range of ideas. Iteration is also very noticeable, since students are building on the ideas expressed by others in the group, using them to enhance their own understanding and expression of this understanding. Such depth would not have been possible had they not reached the catastrophe shelf between the second and third levels of Chaos, and entered another paradigm of discussion.

After graphing the third level discussion, a strange attractor appeared denoting the presence of Chaos. The basins of attraction of Freedom (education as freedom to learn anywhere and from anyone without restrictions of curriculum guides) and Bondage (education as a structured series of content specific competencies to be addressed formally) and the movement of the system around the two basins showed the fine, underlying structure of the chaotic discussion. (see Figure 4.1, p. 72)

It was in this Chaos that the class discovered the secret of *What is education?* They found a time/space where meanings became clearer, understanding became deeper, where new topics followed old, where the impetus for learning was generated by the energy of the group, not because of a one-way flow from teacher to student. The role of the teacher moved from instigator and finder of shelves to participant to observer, but never to disseminator of knowledge or arbiter of solutions and answers.

Summary

Although the three classes were in different domains of education and at different levels, they experienced similar results. In all three classes the students experienced a bonding and a sense of community that had not existed in many other classes. There was more participation on the part of all the students, especially on the part of the male students who tend to shy away from discussion forums. As the students became more involved in their learning, their creativity became evident. Their work tended to be more thoughtful, to involve them in deeper considerations of the issues. They also began to initiate discussions of aspects of the topic at hand that interested them. They became very supportive of each other, trading notes, forming study groups, and bringing supplementary materials to each other.

In taking over the responsibility for their own learning, they also took on the responsibility for moving the learning forward during class meetings, often taking over the class entirely, turning it into a seminar rather than a lecture. The instructors were not ignored, but their roles changed. From instructors and lecturers at the beginning to whom the students looked for information and evaluation, they became facilitators and "boundary keepers" guiding the discussions only insofar as they seemed to get away from the topics to be discussed. Their final role, however, seemed to be as full-fledged members of the community, highly respected and valued, but no more so than any other highly respected and valuable member of the group.

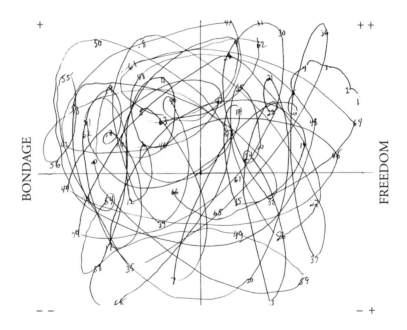

Figure 4.1

CHAPTER 5

CREATING CHAOS AND LOVING IT

Implications for Teachers

For the most part, the teaching/learning process seems to be very straight forward. You teach a concept, your students learn that concept. Except they don't.

There are various explanations for this phenomenon, and up to now, none of them has been very satisfactory. Critical thinking theory has advanced ideas of in-depth learning, Constructivist theory includes ideas of student-directed and student-controlled learning, and brain-based learning theory incorporates the notion of working with the brain in a rich and diverse environment that increases dendritic connections and embeds learning within categories or schema. These three theories alone, however, do not address the diversity and turbulence of today's society and the demands of a changing community. A new theory of learning that incorporates major elements of these three theories, yet creates new guiding principles which lead to a new paradigm is essential. Such a theory looks at learning through the lens of the non-linear science of dynamic systems. The non-linear dynamic learning theory is: one, grounded in constructivist theory; two, brings critical thinking into the constructivist paradigm; three, incorporates current brain research, multiple intelligences and developmental theories; and, four, analyzes the teaching/learning process by applying the principles of Chaos Theory. When learning is viewed as a chaotic process, it is understandable why children learn different things at different times in different ways. When teachers understand that learning is a chaotic process, and that the brain is chaotic in function, they can facilitate learning in a way that is consistent with how the brain works.

Many of the current learning theories such as behavioral learning theory, cognitive learning theory and social learning theory focus on the teaching of skills in a *teacher-controlled* environment. Even when

73

students are given choices, these choices are not really their decisions, but instead are decisions given to them *by the teacher*. Inquiry lessons that are used as models for critical thinking often begin with an "essential question" posed *by the teacher*. And, especially in the behaviorist paradigm, critical thinking skills are taught and required to be mastered before students are allowed to exercise them on their own. Further, the "at-risk" students who are most in need of critical thinking skills are often excluded from the process, because as some see it, they "haven't earned the right", behaviorally or academically to participate in the critical thinking process.

The non-linear dynamic learning theory provides the framework for a brain-friendly classroom and gives teachers sound educational theory for a variety of pedagogical strategies such that students benefit mentally, emotionally and physically from the learning experience. This theory uses critical thinking as a way of developing understanding of content, a strategy that convinces students that learning is a worthwhile activity and that the challenges of substantial inquiry and the pleasure of discovery are theirs to control throughout their lives. (see Figures 5.1 and 5.2, p. 75)

Chaos Theory As a Window to the Learning Process

Chaos Theory supports creative and critical thinking as dynamic processes that are necessary for a comprehensive, intellectually rigorous educational experience. Linking dynamic processes to the creative and critical thinking processes of children in school classrooms requires not an examination of the definitions of critical thinking, which are well established, but instead an examination of chaotic dynamics and their application to brain-based learning processes. In educational terms, applying chaotic dynamics means that learning is a holistic nonlinear process, where input does not equal output, where cause is widely separated from effect, and time is non-reversible.

Compartmentalizing learning into fragments of subject matter also fragments thinking about basic concepts in these disciplines. Thus transfer of these concepts across disciplines is lost, and education is reduced to the acquisition of discrete bits of knowledge that have no relationship to each other.

Figure 5.1

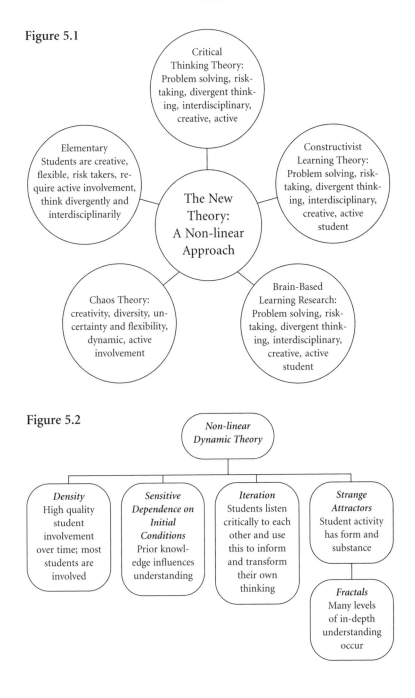

Critical Thinking Theory: Problem solving, risk-taking, divergent thinking, interdisciplinary, creative, active

Elementary Students are creative, flexible, risk takers, require active involvement, think divergently and interdisciplinarily

The New Theory: A Non-linear Approach

Constructivist Learning Theory: Problem solving, risk-taking, divergent thinking, interdisciplinary, creative, active student

Chaos Theory: creativity, diversity, uncertainty and flexibility, dynamic, active involvement

Brain-Based Learning Research: Problem solving, risk-taking, divergent thinking, interdisciplinary, creative, active student

Figure 5.2

Non-linear Dynamic Theory

Density High quality student involvement over time; most students are involved

Sensitive Dependence on Initial Conditions Prior knowledge influences understanding

Iteration Students listen critically to each other and use this to inform and transform their own thinking

Strange Attractors Student activity has form and substance

Fractals Many levels of in-depth understanding occur

Research has shown that optimum conditions for learning require active involvement of students in their own learning, an interdisciplinary approach, inclusion of the creative arts, and both dialogical and dialectical thinking. Research has also shown that critical and creative thinking by their very nature create new neural pathways and multiply dendritic connections. It has also shown that when the brain is not actively involved, neural pathways disappear and thus actual brain damage occurs. It tells us that brain functions are chaotic in design and that the brain works best in a chaotic environment.

It makes sense, then, that Chaos Theory affords the greatest opportunity to understand the manifestations of complex functions that involve learning.

One of the most interesting (and frustrating) aspects of the teaching and learning process is the circumstance where what is *taught* is not what is *learned*. Every teacher has had the experience of planning a wonderful lesson about something very important, and then when asking the students what they understand, finding out that the information in the lesson was converted into something entirely different in the children's minds. This is not a mystery when the learning process is viewed through the combined lenses of brain-based learning and chaos theory. Children assume that what a teacher is talking about is what they are attending to, and they try to fit this new information into existing schema. In chaos theory this has to do with sensitive dependence on initial conditions. What this means is that where a student is in the process of assimilation or accommodation in the development of schema when they encounter new information largely determines what that student will understand about that information. (see Figure 5.3, p. 77)

However, this is just one aspect of sensitive dependence on initial conditions. This principle of learning also leads to diversity of outcomes. This means that when a group of students is presented with the same information or experiences, there will be a wide variety of educational outcomes and these outcomes will be different in part because of the prior knowledge of each student. In true chaotic form, these outcomes are entirely unpredictable.

For example, the investigation of dinosaurs in second grade can lead to a Ph.D. in anthropology later which can result in groundbreaking research in paleontology; or, the linking of math and sci-

Figure 5.3

> **Sensitive Dependence on
> Initial Conditions**
> A principle of Chaos Theory that states
> that small variances can multiply to a
> point of crisis.

> **Educationally Speaking**
> A principle of the Non-linear Learning
> Theory that states that small variances
> of prior knowledge can create wide
> diversity in the understanding of con-
> cepts by students.

> **In the Classroom**
> Students at different levels of prior
> knowledge will understand at different
> level when new information is given to
> them.

ence in a project in fifth grade can lead to sudden insight into the way
numbers and charts and graphs guide the understanding of the way
our society works in the real world.

On a less positive but important note, sensitive dependence on initial conditions can explain what we now call the problem learner, or
at-risk child. A child enters school in a classroom where certain
knowledge is a given for most of the students, and because it takes
time to create the necessary schema to embed the new knowledge that
is being given to her, she ends the first year of school in a far different state of understanding than her peers.

Another aspect of sensitive dependence on initial conditions is that
of intelligences and learning styles. In a classroom that favors verbal/lin-
guistic and logical/mathematical intelligences over any other, and mastery learning styles over any other (which are the majority of classrooms
today) a student who enters the learning process through another intelligence and/or uses a learning style not valued, is highly likely to have a
vastly different learning experience than others in the classroom. In the
view of most brain-based learning researchers, this destroys neural

pathways, causes a sloughing off of brain cells, and does actual damage to the developing brain of a student. Further, any classroom that does not utilize the full strength of the brain to engage the student in the learning process by appealing to critical thinking as a way of understanding curriculum does further damage by creating neural pathways that lead to habits of learning that are at the lowest level of Bloom's taxonomy, e.g. memorization of discrete facts. Because the brain categorizes and embeds new information within schema or categories, the lack of categories, or the lack of the choice to use a preferred intelligence for processing new information either by accommodation or assimilation will result in either the embedding of the new information into inappropriate schema and therefore a complete misunderstanding of the concept, or the refusal of the brain to embed the information anywhere.

Using a knowledge of sensitive dependence on initial conditions in the classroom and incorporating such strategies as a KWL chart (see Figure 5.4, p. 79) to access prior knowledge enables a teacher to create choices for students that will use their already created schema, and facilitate the process of accommodation and assimilation that is necessary for understanding. Further, by allowing students' choices in the methods they use to process their knowledge and by valuing their choices, the teacher can begin to understand the diversity of learning styles and intelligences that her students bring. The students' styles and intelligences create rich, varied and interdisciplinary units of study that are student-directed and student controlled, thereby maximizing the learning that takes place. (see Figure 5.5, p. 79)

What Is a Catastrophe Shelf and How Do We Get Students on One?

Catastrophe Shelves happen all the time. We just don't always recognize them when they occur and most of the time we don't call them that. However, catastrophe shelves are essential to learning, and teachers who are interested in having students understand concepts at the deepest level know how to create them. They also know how to get students to go over the shelf and plunge deeper into understanding.

Piaget theorized that a period of disequilibrium precedes a period of equilibrium (or understanding of a concept) and that this dise-

Figure 5.4

Strategies for Using a KWL Chart

- *Show and Tell:* When introducing a new unit, have students bring something in that will be a part of the unit, and have them discuss it. Then, when you introduce the KWL chart, they will be able to contribute more fully to the K and W parts of the chart. For example, when beginning a unit on Plants, have students bring in their favorite plant from home, or a plant from their yard. Next, take a nature walk around the school and bring back leaves, samples of bark or take digital photos of plants you find on your walk for students to talk about. Introduce some of the vocabulary you will be using, such as leaves, stems, bark, roots, buds, etc. Even though most students have some prior knowledge about plants, this helps them focus their prior knowledge and begin to use the vocabulary of the study.

- *Think-Pair-Share:* Have students create their own personal KWL chart, writing in the K and W parts only. Then students will share their chart with a partner and combine the two charts. Next the pair will share with another pair, and again combine the two charts into one. Finally, the groups will contribute to a class chart, combining all the group charts into one, then adding anything else they may have thought of during the discussion.

Figure 5.5

Strategies to Create Prior Knowledge When Your Students Don't Have Any

- *Field Trips:* If you are planning a unit on a topic about which your students have little or no prior knowledge, take a field trip to a place that will give them hands-on experience. For example, if you are studying the ocean, and your students have never been to the beach, take them on a field trip there before you begin the unit. Or if you are planning a unit on farm animals for a group of inner city students, take them to the farm first.

- *Shared Experiences:* When some students have some prior knowledge but others do not, have the students with the prior knowledge share at some length their experiences and understanding of the topic. They or their parents can bring in scrapbooks, photos, or other objects to enhance the sharing.

- *Research:* Form groups of students to research various concepts within a topic and report back to the whole class. List important facts on the KWL chart under K. Students can then generate questions for the W part of the chart which can comprise much of the unit. For example, when students know very little about Canada, one group of students might research the climate and weather in Canada, another group can create a map, etc. With such information the class can now generate better questions about Canada.

Figure 5.6

> *Chaos Theory: Catastrophe Shelf*
> The point at which variables combine
> in such a way as to produce suddenly
> different behavior, and entering as it
> were a parallel universe with noticeably
> different behavior, and with noticeably
> different time/space.

> *Everyday Example*
> A small child sees a circus clown for the
> first time. As long as the clown stays
> some distance away, the child is enter-
> tained and laughs. But when the clown
> approaches just one step too close, the
> child abruptly begins to cry and runs
> away. Delight has changed to fright.

> *Classroom Example*
> The "Ah Ha!" moment: A child has
> been listening to several explanations
> about a concept without getting it.
> The teacher tries one more time with
> another different variation of the
> concept. Suddenly the child's eyes light
> up, and it is clear that understanding
> has happened.

quilibrium is essential for learning to move from an elemental understanding to in-depth understanding. When students notice an
anomaly or something about what they thought they knew that does-
n't quite make sense, they begin to question their original understanding. Curiosity and the quest for making sense out of data that
is contrary to their prior knowledge are the driving forces that impel
students to dig deeper into a concept and to come to an understanding, or equilibrium, about it.

Chaos Theory speaks to this in the form of catastrophe shelves and
bifurcation points. A bifurcation point is where something that has
been going along in one direction suddenly divides itself and goes off

Figure 5.7

Curiosity about the
anomaly and trying to
make sense of the new
materials, data and
experiences

Equilibrium or
understanding of a
concept

*Introduction of new
data, materials or
experiences or noticing
an anomaly creates a*
bifurcation point *or a*
catastrophe shelf

in two different directions. For example, two students are working
together on a research project. One student remains quite interested
in the original line of research, but the other student comes across
some information that makes her think about the research in an entirely different way. She and her partner now begin to develop two
very different perspectives on their research, and the papers they finally write, although they started out on the same topic, are very different in their conclusions. The bifurcation point was caused by
something the second student read or data that the second student
interpreted that led her to the different point of view. This bifurcation point corresponds to Piaget's explanation of disequilibrium
caused by the introduction of an anomaly or contrary data. In both
explanations, the encounter led to further exploration of the topic
which can, under the guidance of a skillful facilitator of learning, lead
to greater understanding. (see Figure 5.7, above)

However, recognizing the necessity of the catastrophe shelves and
the usefulness of the bifurcation points as explanations for student

learning is only the first step. A vital part of the Nonlinear Dynamic Theory of Learning has to do with the role of the teacher.

In a traditional classroom, the teacher takes the stance of The Expert Who Knows, and the students take the role of the Empty Vessels That Are Ready to be Filled. The traditional pedagogy is that of lecture, maybe question-and-answer, quiz, and final examination.

In the Chaotic Classroom, however, the role of the teacher is that of Facilitator of Learning, Asker of Good Questions, and Provider of materials, data and experiences, and the role of the student is that of Sense-Maker and Constructor of Knowledge. In addition, the teacher creates Catastrophe Shelves and Bifurcation Points in the form of anomalies, confusions, and evidence contrary to *a priori* knowledge. Thus the role of teacher as facilitator becomes teacher as catalyst of learning.

As far as we know at this point in the research, chaos exists in three levels. *Level one* refers to systems that iterate to a single point, zero. Such a system returns to its initial conditions time after time. One example is a rubber band that returns to its original shape after being stretched, or a guitar string that remains in tune for some time. Another example is a discussion that comes to consensus after a period of consideration of alternative perspectives or solutions. This is not entropy which refers to systems which iterate to an infinite number of random points. Figure 5.8 on page 83 shows a mathematically created single point attractor retrieved from www.fractalwisdom.com/FractalWisdom/fourattr.html.

One example of this level is a discussion in an elementary classroom about a proposed classroom project involving all students. Perhaps many ideas are suggested, and the discussion revolves around the pros and cons of each one, but in the end there can be only one project to which all must compromise. Students invoke their prior knowledge of each idea (sensitive dependence on initial conditions) and listen to the advantages of other ideas proffered by other students and use this information to make an informed decision (iteration) about the best proposal for this particular project (level one chaos). This differs from the discussion which entropies, because in that kind of discussion, the group never reaches consensus, nothing gets decided, no one listens to anyone else (iteration does not take place) and the whole idea fizzles out. (see Figure 5.9, p. 83)

Figure 5.8

Figure 5.9

Level One Chaos
A characteristic of a chaotic system in
which all points when iterated cycle to a
single point or zero. This differs from
entropy in which all the points in the
system when iterated cycle to an infinite
number of random points.

Educationally Speaking
Level one chaos in an elementary
classroom is a characteristic of a project
or discussion in which all the students
involved reach consensus after
exploring many different perspectives
or solutions.

In the Classroom
Students are working on the solution
to a word problem in mathematics.
Several students each propose various
ways to solve the problem, but after
some discussion of the pros and cons of
each method, one is chosen as the best
way to solve the problem.

Figure 5.10

---

*Strategies for Creating Level One Chaos in an
Elementary School Classroom*

Instead of having students memorize formulas to solve mathematical problems, allow them the time to figure out as many ways as possible to solve them, and then decide which way is the most efficient or more likely to produce a correct answer.

Call class meetings to resolve problems that have occurred in the classroom, on the playground or on the school bus and allow students to discuss possible solutions and then decide on the best one.

Give students a research project, for example, the water cycle, and allow the group to decide how to do the research and how to present the information. They might choose to create a puppet show, write a song about it, develop a power point presentation, or some other way, but the group comes to consensus about what they are doing.

The *second level* is a chaotic system that cycles between two points, often called a damped and driven system. A familiar example of this kind of system is the air conditioning in your home that is controlled by a thermostat. When the heat builds up to a certain point, the air conditioner cuts on and runs until the heat is lowered to a certain, predetermined level. The system cycles endlessly between the two points. Figure 5.11 page 85 illustrates this type of attractor. It was retrieved from www.fractalwisdom.com/FractalWisdom/fourattr.html.

When students in an elementary school classroom consider alternative ways to solve problems, for example, and find equally good solutions they agree that both (or more) methods will work just as well.

Another example would be when students are discussing various interpretations of an event, such as cause and effect. When they discover multiple causes that can equally cause the effect, through discussion and exploration of the implications of each cause, they may finally agree to disagree. Thus each student proffers a particular point of view (sensitive dependence on initial conditions), listens to other students' perspectives and uses these perspectives to inform and change or inform and confirm their original perspective (iteration) and thus come

Figure 5.11

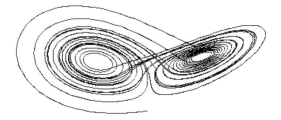

Figure 5.12

> *Level Two Chaos*
> A characteristic of a chaotic system that
> cycles between two points without
> cycling to a single point or zero.

> *Educationally Speaking*
> A characteristic of the consideration of
> two or more equally valid perspectives,
> points of view or solutions wherein
> consensus is not desired.

> *In the Classroom*
> Students are trying to decide how best
> to display the physical characteristics of
> insects. One group wants to create a
> papier mache model and the other
> group wants to display a diagram.
> They decide to do both.

to realize that there can be several equally good solutions (level two chaos). (see Figure 5.12, above and Figure 5.13, p. 86)

The *third level* is characterized by a system that moves through many points in many dimensions, creating a robustness that is not easily perturbed thus creating its own time/space, and generativeness or creativeness that can at any point create a different time/space. (see Figure 5.14, p. 87) It is unpredictable locally but predictable globally. The energy that is created in this third level comes from its characteristic far-from-equilibrium properties, and this energy sustains it over

Figure 5.13

Strategies for Creating Level Two Chaos in an
Elementary School Classroom

Use open-ended questions to encourage students to critically listen to the points of view of others.

Encourage students to find many different ways to solve problems and to try using several of them.

Rewrite a familiar story from the point of view of one of the characters who is not telling the story, i.e the story of the three little pigs from the point of view of the pigs' mother.

---

long periods of time. Rather than tending to entropy, the system is inclined to suddenly change direction or focus and this new focus now becomes robust in a new time/space. This sudden creative movement of the system that changes the focus and direction of the old system is the same movement described when encountering a catastrophe shelf.

When students in an elementary school classroom work together on research or other projects, or come together for a Socratic discussion, they tend to approach it from their own perspective (sensitive dependence on initial conditions). Their *a priori* knowledge may be in error or incomplete such that their understanding of a concept is misconstrued. When this prior knowledge is challenged, they go through a period of what Piaget has termed "disequilibrium," and what is called chaotic cognition in the Non-linear Theory of Learning. This is a time when students receive information that is at odds with previously held information which causes confusion or questioning of assumptions or beliefs about a concept. At that time, clearing up the confusion and answering the questions that are generated become the prime motivation for the study, and as the confusion clears and questions are answered, new topics for inquiry are generated. Motivation for the activity comes from within the confusion and questioning rather than from outside, such as teacher prompting or quest for grades or test scores. Because of the confusion and questioning that is generated, schema that were previously developed about the concept are reorganized to accommodate the new infor-

Figure 5.14   **The picture below was retrieved from www.jracademy. com/FractalPictures.**

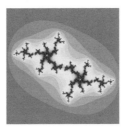

Figure 5.15

> *Third Level or Deep Chaos*
> A characteristic of a chaotic system in which many variables work together to create a system that has a structure that supports original, creative movement of the points and which is capable of generating new systems

> *Educationally Speaking*
> A characteristic of a classroom that works on its own to solve problems and generate information and that will generate new topics to study without requiring outside direction or motivation.

> *In the Classroom*
> The study of a particular topic becomes student directed and motivated by excitement of the study itself, and leads to another topic for study.

mation, thus learning is advanced and understanding of the concept is both broadened and deepened. And in the process, more questions and more evocative confusion is generated creating the motivation for exploration of a new topic. (see Figure 5.14, above)

In the classroom, this process can look very random and many teachers are concerned about students being "off task" when in

Figure 5.16

> *Strategies for getting to the Third Level of Chaos in an*
> *Elementary School Classroom*
>
> Use Socratic discussions about issues of real importance to students to help students create understanding of content.
>
> Allow students to decide on topics of study through which the teacher will facilitate the understanding of required competencies such as reading for comprehension, or learning addition or multiplication.
>
> Give students ample time to explore ideas and concepts in an interdisciplinary setting without restraints on their explorations or parameters on how they demonstrate their learning.
>
> Use multiple approaches to facilitating comprehension.

essence the confusion and questioning are part of the process of learning. However, this is not true if the task given the students does not require complex thinking. Students cannot be expected to experience productive confusion and questioning if they are only answering dull and lower level questions at the end of an equally dull and lower level chapter in a basal text. Of course they will be off task!

Summary

Creating Chaos in a classroom is not as difficult at it may seem, and can be incredibly beneficial to all students. Teachers who are dedicated to deep understanding of content rather than superficial learning in order to generate high test scores will find that a chaotic dynamic and the critical and creative thinking that it fosters is exciting, engaging and productive even as it appears random from the outside. Because the brain is nonlinear in its functioning, a nonlinear dynamic in the classroom can produce an optimal environment for learning.

References

Davis-Seaver, Jane (2001). *Critical thinking in young children.* Lewiston, NY: Mellen.

Gleick, James (1987). *Chaos: Making a new science.* New York: Penguin.

Jensen, Eric (1997). *Brain compatible strategies.* San Diego: The Brain Store.

Jensen, Eric. What is brain-based learning. http://www.jlcbrain.com/BBLearn/whatis.asp. Retrieved 7/26/07.

Hiley, B.J. and Peat, F. David, eds. (1987). *Quantum implications: Essays in honour of David Bohm.* London: Routledge.

Hooper, J. & Teresi, D. (1986). *The three pound universe.* New York: Dell.

John-Steiner, V. (1985). *Notebooks of the mind: Explorations of thinking.* New York: Harper & Row.

Lackney, John. *12 design principles based on brain-based learning research.* DesignShare: The International Forum for Innovative Schools. Retrieved 2/17/2007 from www.designshare.com/Research/BrainBased/Learn98.htm.

Paul, Richard (1993). *Critical thinking: What every person needs to survive in a rapidly changing world.* Rohnert Park, CA: Foundation for Critical Thinking.

Petree, Judy. *History of chaos.* www.newscientist.com Retrieved 12.03.

Provost, J. and Anchors, S., eds. (1987). *Application of the Myers-Briggs Type Indicator in Higher Education.* Palo Alto, CA: Consulting Psychologists Press.

Ratey, John, Conference notes from the Learning and the Brain conference, Cambridge, Mass., 2002.

Silver, H., Stron, R., and Perini, M. (2000). *So each may learn: Integrating learning styles and multiple intelligences.* Alexandria, VA: ASCD.

Wolf, Maryanne. Paper presented at the Learning and the Brain conference, Cambridge, Mass., 2002.

Index